INDUSTRIAL
CYBERSECURITY

A PRACTICAL APPROACH TO OT PROTECTION

Anand Shinde / Bipin Lokegaonkar

With profound gratitude, I dedicate this book to Shree Mahadev Shambho, the orchestrator of my life's journey. Your blessings infuse every word, guiding the pages with same grace that has illuminated my path.

!!! Jai Mahakaal !!!

ABOUT AUTHOR

Bipin Lokegaonkar is a cybersecurity expert with over two decades of experience in SOC, SIEM, VAPT, data security, application security, cloud security, OT security, and IDAM. Throughout his career, Bipin has worked with prominent companies such as Tata Communications, Adani, Ernst & Young-UKI, Wipro, Capgemini, NTT, and Netmagic, where he has gained extensive industry expertise and honed his skills in developing comprehensive security strategies.

Bipin's deep understanding of both technical and managerial aspects of cybersecurity has made him a sought-after advisor and thought leader in the field. He is committed to staying ahead of evolving cyber threats and continuously improving security practices to protect critical infrastructures and sensitive data. Passionate about sharing his knowledge, Bipin frequently engages in speaking events and workshops, where he educates and inspires fellow professionals. This book on OT security is a testament to his dedication to the field. The book also offers practical insights and actionable strategies for protecting operational technology environments, drawing from Bipin's vast experience and in-depth knowledge.

Bipin's commitment to excellence, continuous learning, and innovation in cybersecurity has earned him recognition as a thought leader in the industry. His book aims to be an essential resource for professionals seeking to enhance their understanding and implementation of OT security, providing them with the tools and knowledge needed to navigate the complexities of securing operational technology.

Anand Shinde is an accomplished author of cyber security books and is a dedicated cybersecurity expert with extensive experience in diverse cybersecurity technologies. Throughout his career, Anand has made significant contributions to the cybersecurity community, both through his professional engagements with multinational corporations across India, Poland, Ireland, and the USA, and through his educational initiatives. He is renowned for his ability to translate complex cyber security challenges into comprehensible solutions, making him a valued figure in both industry and academic circles.

Anand also dedicates his expertise to mentoring the next generation of cybersecurity professionals. He actively participates as a cyber security career counsellor and student mentor at MID ADT University, Pune and other education institutions in India and Ireland, where he guides students with a blend of real-world experience and theoretical knowledge.

With numerous awards under his belt, Anand's impact on the field is undeniable. His work not only educates but also inspires action, contributing to a safer and more secure cyber environment for all.

For further engagement with Anand Shinde and to explore his extensive insights, visit his website at https://cyberauthor.tech/

CONTENTS

01 OPERATIONAL TECHNOLOGY SYSTEMS

1.1 INTRODUCTION: IMPORTANCE OF INDUSTRIES IN MODERN LIFE

Industries are the backbone of our society, impacting our lives and economic well-being in different ways. Their influence goes beyond making goods and services; they shape the way our economies work, our structures, and how we take care of the environment at their very heart. Industries are giving new opportunities for jobs. Bring about innovation that drives us forward in providing products and services—from the food we eat to the clothes we wear to how we connect globally through transportation. In addition to their importance industries also make a contribution to society by offering employment opportunities, education and healthcare services that improve the lives of people around the world. Industries have a role in protecting the environment and conserving resources to ensure a future for generations to come.

In todays interconnected world, industries are increasingly relying on technologies such as systems, electrical machinery and digital automation to run efficiently. The integration of Operational Technology (OT) that manages infrastructures like power grids, water treatment facilities and manufacturing plants has become crucial in this advancement. As OT closely merges with Information Technology (IT) it becomes vulnerable to cyber threats that are always evolving—highlighting the need, for strong cybersecurity measures. we can protect the pillars of our society by improving occupational therapy services and bolstering industry resilience thus, ensuring progress, societal development and environmental conservation, for generations.

1.2 OT OVERVIEW

Operational Technology (OT) encompasses both hardware and software that directly interact with the world. This technology plays a role in sectors like transportation, energy, manufacturing and utilities by overseeing and managing physical devices, processes and infrastructure. In simple understanding OT systems consist of interconnected control elements working together to achieve objectives. These elements are divided into two sections: the process section that generates output and the controller section that ensures the system functions within defined parameters.

With time, Operational Technology has progressed by integrating Information Technology (IT) features into these systems. This development has led to innovations such as transportation systems, intelligent buildings and the Internet of Things (IoT). These advancements signify a shift towards blending physical systems to enhance efficiency and productivity.

Operational Technology-Based Systems and their Interdependencies

Operational Technology (OT) is an essential part of many vital industries that support society. From chemical manufacturing to healthcare, energy supply to emergency services, OT systems play an important role in ensuring the smooth running of facilities and services critical to societal well-being. This topic tries to educate OT, its applications, and its importance in guaranteeing the resilience of key infrastructures.

Sectors Dependent on OT

OT Based Systems

| Chemical Sector | Energy Sector | Nuclear Sector | Dams Sector |

| Critical Manufacturing Sector | Health Care Sector | Transportation Sector | Oil & Gas Sector |

| Defense Industrial Base Sector | Food & Agriculture Sector | Emergency Services Sector | Water & Wastewater Sector |

OT has a wide range of applications, each of which is crucial to societal stability and safety. Notable sectors are:

- **Chemical Sector:** Controls the manufacturing and distribution of chemical compounds.

- **Healthcare Sector:** Manages the operational efficiency of medical institutions.

- **Energy Sector:** Oversees energy generation, transmission, and distribution.
- **Water and Wastewater Sector:** Manages water treatment and distribution networks.
- **Transportation Systems:** Controls the operations of rail, aviation, and maritime transportation.
- **Emergency Services:** Coordinates crisis response actions.
- **Food and Agriculture:** Facilitates the supply chain from farm to table.
- **Defense Industrial Base:** Ensures national defense capability.
- **Dams and Critical Industrial:** Responsible for the integrity and operation of dams and key industrial operations.
- **Automobile Sector:** Manages vehicle manufacturing processes, integrating robotics and supply chain logistics to ensure efficiency and safety.
- **National Critical Infrastructure:** Includes essential systems such as energy, water, transportation, communications, and financial services. These sectors are vital for national security, public health, and economic stability. Protecting them involves robust cybersecurity measures, resilient protocols, and continuous monitoring to prevent and mitigate disruptions.

The Collaboration of OT Systems

OT systems are inseparably linked, and their functions frequently rely on shared communication networks and protocols, such as wireless systems and 3G, 4G, or 5G technologies. This interconnection, although improving operating efficiency and flexibility, poses significant weaknesses. A breakdown in the communication network, for example, might cause extensive disruptions across many sectors, highlighting the importance of effective OT system security.

Importance of OT System Protection

The risk of flow failures across interconnected OT systems highlights the vital necessity for strict security measures. Blackouts or operational failures in one sector can have far-reaching consequences, including medical services, transportation, and emergency response. Protecting these systems requires not just defending specific sectors but also maintaining the continuity and dependability of vital services that society relies on.

1.3 EVOLUTION OF OPERATIONAL TECHNOLOGY (OT)

The Industrial Revolution was a turning point in history that greatly transformed society. Prior to industrialisation, the majority of people resided in areas working as farmers or craftsmen with social structures remaining largely unchanged for generations. However, the rise of factories mass-producing goods prompted a migration to centres in search of job opportunities. This transition brought about shifts in lifestyle, employment patterns and social interactions, leading to the adoption of technologies and ideas that hastened societal changes. In essence, the Industrial Revolution symbolised the transition from products to production.

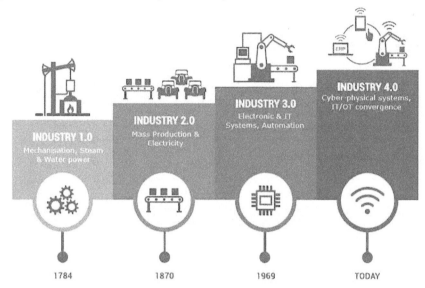

This industrial progression narrates a tale of ingenuity and technological advancement that has deeply impacted our way of life. It has left its mark on societies over centuries, with each stage introducing revolutionary transformations in various industries. From the steam-driven factories of the Industrial Revolution to the interconnected systems of Industry 4.0, every era has heralded groundbreaking developments in manufacturing, transportation and communication. Defined below is the hierarchal order of how the industry has evolved with time.

Industry 1.0: The Birth of Mechanization (Late 18th Century - Mid 19th Century)

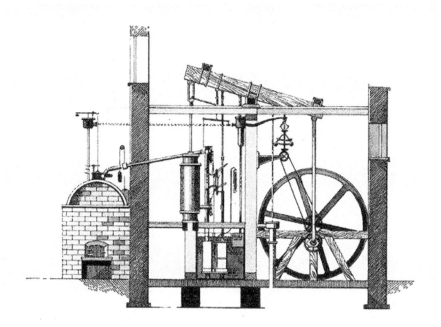

The first industrial revolution, known as Industry 1.0, started in the late 18th century and marked a significant shift from manual labour to mechanization. Key inventions such as the steam engine, spinning jenny, and power loom transformed textile manufacturing, greatly increasing production and leading to urbanization. This era was largely influenced by steam power, enhancing both productivity and production volume. Notable developments included the invention of the flying shuttle in 1733, which simplified the cloth weaving process, the establishment of the first textile mill in the US in 1790, and the patenting of the cotton gin in 1794. This transition from agrarian to industrial economies signalled the onset of modern industry, but it also introduced challenges like poor working conditions and labour exploitation.

Industry 2.0: The Age of Electricity and Electronics (Late 19th Century - Early 20th Century)

Industry 2.0 saw the widespread adoption of electricity as a source of power, a development that further revolutionised manufacturing processes. Electric motors replaced steam engines, offering greater efficiency and precision in industrial operations. Factories became increasingly electrified, allowing for more flexible and adaptable production lines. The introduction of assembly lines, pioneered by Henry Ford's production of automobiles, further revolutionised manufacturing. These streamlined workflows, characterised by synchronised movements and repetitive tasks, drastically reduced production time and increased output, leading to a surge in consumer goods and a transformation of the global economy.

Electricity's versatility allowed for greater control and precision in manufacturing processes. Businesses became more profitable and agile, capable of responding swiftly to changes in consumer preferences. Innovations in electronic assembly techniques further enhanced production efficiency, reducing the cost of producing electronic components and devices. Industry 2.0 improved industrial output and transformed everyday life as electrical appliances and lighting became commonplace in households.

Industry 3.0: The Age of Automation and Computers (Mid 20th Century - Late 20th Century)

Industry 3.0 emerged in the 1970s, marking a significant shift towards factory automation. This phase involved replacing human labor with intelligent machines, programs, and algorithms that enhanced speed and efficiency in production. This era signified a transformation from mechanized and analog systems to digital and automated operations within factories and broader industries. Stemming from the mechanization and mass production characteristic of Industry 2.0, Industry 3.0 was shaped by the late 20th century through the integration of electronics and information technology. This shift led to revolutionary changes in factory operations, with automation replacing manual labor in many repetitive tasks and robotic systems enhancing efficiency and precision.

Industry 3.0 dramatically transformed operational processes in manufacturing sectors. It improved operational efficiency through automation and robotics, created safer working environments, and shifted the workforce focus from manual tasks to more strategic, IT-oriented roles. It also initiated the rise of smart factories, where decisions are driven by real-time data. This progress set the stage for Industry 4.0, which further integrates advanced AI, machine learning, and cyber-physical systems into manufacturing processes.

Industry 4.0: The Age of Connectivity and Digital Twins (Late 20th Century - 21st Century)

We are currently in the midst of the Fourth Industrial Revolution, also known as "Industry 4.0." This phase is characterized by integrating information and communication technologies into industrial processes. Building on the innovations of the Third Industrial Revolution, this era extends existing computerized production systems by adding network connectivity and creating a digital counterpart, or "digital twin," online. These systems can communicate with other devices and report on their status, marking a significant advancement in production automation. The result is the creation of "cyber-physical production systems" and smart factories, where production systems, components, and people interact seamlessly through networks, enabling nearly autonomous production. Industry 4.0 offers remarkable possibilities for enhancing factory operations. For example, machines can now predict their own failures and initiate maintenance automatically, and logistics systems can adapt to changes in production schedules on their own.

This revolution is also transforming the workplace. Industry 4.0 connects individuals into more efficient networks, enhancing productivity through digitalization. This shift allows for more agile dissemination of vital information to the right person at the right time. With the increased use of digital devices in factories and on-site, maintenance professionals can access necessary equipment documentation and service history more promptly and accurately.

This efficiency shift enables maintenance workers to focus on solving problems rather than spending time searching for the technical information they require.

1.4 IT AND OT CONVERGENCE:

The convergence of IT (Information Technology) and OT (Operational Technology) means that events in the real world can now interact seamlessly with digital networks. Both IT and OT are crucial for transmitting information, storing data, and supporting the core processes of many businesses. By integrating these systems, organisations can send data collected from OT processes directly to their IT networks, enabling a unified approach to system monitoring. This merging of IT and **OT has** recently made it possible to achieve unprecedented levels of efficiency and innovation. It not only eliminates barriers that hinder productivity and growth but also opens up many new opportunities for organisations willing to adopt this change. While the integration of these two domains offers significant advantages like streamlined operations and improved decision-making based on data, it also introduces several challenges that need to be managed carefully.

Benefits of IT/OT Convergence

IT/OT convergence allows for more direct control and comprehensive monitoring of complex systems from anywhere in the world. This improves efficiency for workers and enhances decision-making as organisations gain access to real-time insights from converged data. Industries such as manufacturing, transportation, and mining are increasingly adopting this integrated approach.

Key Benefits:

- **Unified Departments:** IT and OT departments collaborate more closely, sharing expertise to manage the integrated technology effectively.
- **Improved Cybersecurity:** By merging IT and OT systems into a single unified environment, security is enhanced across both platforms, reducing vulnerabilities.

- **Cost Efficiency:** Convergence leads to lower development, operational, and support costs. Predictive maintenance enabled by IoT devices also reduces unplanned downtime.

- **Faster Market Entry:** Products and technologies reach the market more quickly due to streamlined processes.

- **Enhanced Compliance:** Adding IT capabilities to OT improves visibility, management, and auditing, helping meet regulatory standards more effectively.

- **Advanced Automation and Visibility:** OT can now transmit real-time maintenance data, improving automation and operational visibility.

- **Optimized Resource Use:** Systems operate more efficiently in response to actual needs, enhancing energy and resource management.

- **Streamlined Asset Management:** A common management approach allows for better visibility and control of all IT and OT assets.

Challenges of IT/OT Convergence

A significant challenge in IT/OT convergence is ensuring security. Many OT systems were not originally designed for standard communication or remote access, increasing the risk of cyber threats. These systems might not receive regular updates, and their widespread distribution can make critical infrastructure vulnerable to attacks, including industrial espionage and sabotage.

Additional Challenges Include:

- **Process Convergence:** Merging previously separate IT and OT departments to manage converged technologies can be difficult, requiring significant organizational restructuring.

- **Secure IoT Implementation:** IoT projects often lack clear ownership, which can lead to communication breakdowns and security gaps, especially in organizations where departments are siloed.

- **Training:** There is a gap in standardized training for OT workers on networked technology, leading to potential compatibility and security issues. New certifications like Cisco Certified Network Associate Industrial IoT are starting to address this gap.

- **Integration with Existing Systems:** There is a temptation to replace old technologies rather than integrate them with new IT solutions, which can undermine the cost-efficiency benefits of convergence.

1.5 CYBERSECURITY ATTACKS ON OT NETWORKS:

In industries like energy, manufacturing, and transportation, Operational Technology (OT) systems that manage processes are increasingly susceptible to cyberattacks. These attacks can lead to severe consequences, including operational disruptions, financial losses, physical damage, and even loss of life. The range and types of threat actors targeting OT systems have expanded, moving from primarily nation-state adversaries now to include groups, hacktivists, and individual hackers. In the IT realm, there's a common saying: "It's not about IF it will happen, but WHEN."

The field of Industrial Control Systems (ICS) and OT has experienced numerous security incidents, though many remain undisclosed. Some notable instances include:

OT Infrastructure Attacks

1. **2003: Davis Besse Power Plant and SQL Slammer:** In 2003, the Davis Besse power plant in Ohio was compromised by the SQL Slammer worm through an unauthorized internet connection. This incident forced the plant to shut down some operations, underscoring the vulnerability of even isolated systems.

2. **2010: Stuxnet:** Stuxnet, developed by the United States and Israel, targeted Iran's Natanz Nuclear facility in 2010. This cyberattack was designed to disrupt the centrifuges in Iran's nuclear weapons program, marking a significant moment in cyber warfare history.

3. **2015 & 2016: Ukrainian Blackouts:** Ukraine faced multiple blackouts between 2015 and 2016 due to cyberattacks on their ICS/OT systems. These attacks occurred during winter, demonstrating the severe impact on critical infrastructure.

4. **2017: Trisis/Triton:** In 2017, a cyber group believed to be from Russia targeted a Middle Eastern petrochemical plant. They gained access to the Safety Instrumented System (SIS), which is designed to ensure safety by shutting down the plant during emergencies. The attackers aimed to cause an explosion or significant damage.

5. **2021: Colonial Pipeline:** The Colonial Pipeline was attacked in 2021, initially impacting its IT systems but quickly affecting the OT network that controls the pipeline. This led to the largest gasoline pipeline in the U.S. being shut down for 10 days, highlighting the vulnerability of critical infrastructure to cyber threats.

These events serve as a reminder of the dangers present in the field of operational technology and industrial control systems. They highlight the pressing importance of implementing cybersecurity protocols to defend infrastructure and counter the ever-changing cyber threat environment.

1.6 IT / IOT & OT:

The illustration below displays the positions of IT/IoT/OT and other devices. The green circle indicates the IT devices. While this diagram only depicts a laptop, it could encompass routers, firewalls, Wi-Fi devices, printers and more. The IoT circle represents items that are now connected to the internet, like bulbs and cameras. The lowermost circle features machinery utilised across industries.

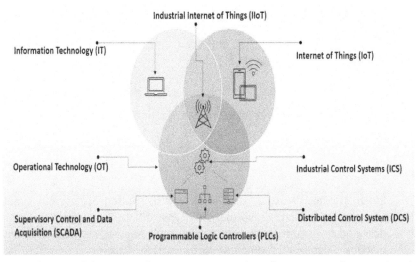

Now, let us delve into the components that form part of Operational Technology (OT) and their respective functions.

PLC:

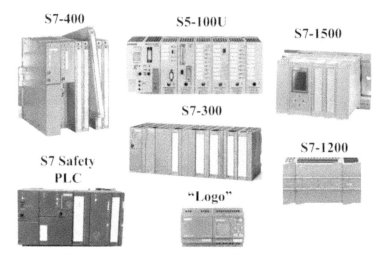

A programmable logic controller (PLC) is a type of computer that is utilized in overseeing operations and machinery. It functions by following a set of commands to automate tasks, such as supervising assembly lines and managing water treatment procedures. The adaptability, dependability and endurance of PLCs make them highly effective in demanding conditions, which is why they are widely favored in manufacturing and other industries.

Introduced in the 1960s as a replacement for relay systems in automotive production, PLCs were initially embraced by companies like General Motors to enhance factory control processes. Over time PLC technology has advanced significantly. Now holds a role, across diverse sectors including manufacturing, energy production, water treatment and more.

HMI:

Human Machine Interface (HMI) refers to panels or dashboards that establish a link between machines, equipment, processes and the operator or engineer.

A common instance of an HMI is a bank's Automated Teller Machine (ATM) allowing users to engage with the bank for withdrawing or depositing money.

MES: A Manufacturing Execution System (MES) is software that connects, monitors and oversees manufacturing operations and data flow within a factory. The main goal of an MES is to improve the effectiveness of manufacturing processes and increase production output. In order to achieve this, an MES. Gathers real-time data at every stage of a product's lifecycle, beginning from order placement to final product delivery.

OT Historian:

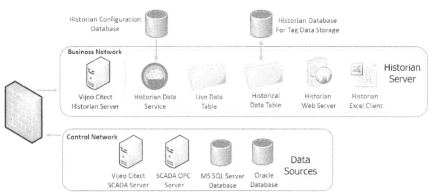

Historian Architecture

A data or process historian, also known as an operational historian or simply "historian," is a specialized type of time-series database software. It is designed primarily to collect and store data related to industrial operations. Historians emerged in the latter half of the 1980s, initially developed to work with industrial automation systems like SCADA (Supervisory Control And Data Acquisition). They were particularly designed toward supporting process manufacturing industries such as oil and gas, chemicals, pharmaceuticals, pipelines, refining, etc.

Today, process historians are utilized broadly across various industries. They serve as crucial tools for performance monitoring, supervisory control, analytics, and quality assurance. These systems enable industrial facility managers, stakeholders, engineers, data scientists, and machinery operators to access data gathered from a range of automated systems and sensors. This data is essential for monitoring performance, tracking processes, or conducting business analytics. Modern historians often include additional functionalities, such as the capability to generate both automated and manual reports. It's important to note that while data historians share similarities with conventional databases like SQL, they are distinct. Historians not only collect raw data but are also typically equipped to process collected data, organize it into reports, and forward it to other storage systems. Essentially, a data historian is a highly specialized time-series database tailored to meet the specific needs of industrial automation.

SCADA:

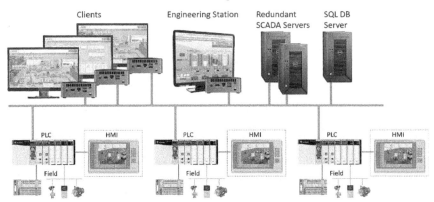

Supervisory Control and Distribution Acquisition (SCADA) is a system used by organizations to oversee and manage their operations from a point. It involves the use of both hardware and software to gather data from sensors and devices process it, and present it in a user manner to operators. Additionally, SCADA includes alarm features that notify operators of any risks. While SCADA is sometimes compared to the Industrial Internet of Things (IIoT), they are not identical. SCADA systems are typically more centralized and tightly connected, whereas IIoT systems offer flexibility and compatibility. In terms of solutions, SCADA providers often offer made packages, whereas IIoT providers may provide an array of hardware and software options.

RTU:

A Remote Terminal Unit (RTU) is an electronically sophisticated device governed by a microprocessor, designed to interface objects in the physical world with a distributed control system or a SCADA (Supervisory Control and Data Acquisition) system. This device facilitates communication by sending telemetry data to a central master system and executing commands received from this supervisory system to manage the connected objects. RTUs may also be referred to as remote telemetry units or remote tele-control units. They play a crucial role in monitoring digital and analog parameters within a field and transmitting this data back to a SCADA Master Station. Additionally, RTUs operate setup software that connects input data streams to output streams, establishes communication protocols, and addresses installation issues in the field.

SIS: In the context of functional safety, a Safety Instrumented System (SIS) comprises an engineered combination of hardware and software controls. It acts as a protective layer designed to shut down chemical, nuclear, electrical, or mechanical systems or specific parts thereof upon the detection of hazardous conditions.

IED: Intelligent Electronic Devices (IEDs) are defined as devices incorporating one or more microprocessors. These devices primarily facilitate the transmission and reception of data or control signals to or from external equipment. Such external devices, in the context of the entire system, may include transducers, relays, and control units, among others. IEDs are considered a crucial component of industrial control systems, extensively employed in advanced power automation.

BMS: A Building Management System (BMS), alternatively known as Building Automation System (BAS) or Building Control System (BCS), functions as a cyber-physical system tasked with supervising and enhancing operations within facilities. Essential components of a BMS encompass systems for heating, ventilation, and air conditioning (HVAC), alongside lighting management. Security functionalities are also integral, featuring access card systems, surveillance cameras, and various alarm mechanisms.

DCS:

Distributed Control Systems

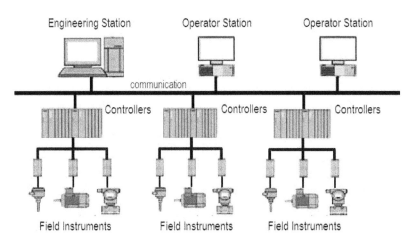

A distributed control system (DCS) is a system that controls a process or plant using autonomous controllers spread across the system. Unlike control systems, with controllers in a location, DCS distributes controllers throughout the plant for better reliability and cost efficiency. This setup localizes control functions, near the process plant while enabling monitoring and supervision.

CPS: A Cyber-Physical System (CPS), or an intelligent system, involves a setup where specialized software is in control of a physical device or mechanism. These setups integrate hardware components, like sensors and actuators, with the software elements that operate them. Typically, these are also recognized as embedded systems, but with a stronger emphasis on the symbiosis between software and physical entities. Common applications of such systems are found in power grids, driverless cars, health tracking for patients, systems for industrial automation, robotics, management of waste systems, and aircraft autopilot functionalities.

IoT:

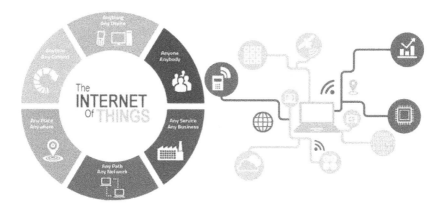

The Internet of Things (IoT) concept connects physical objects to the internet. Equipped with sensors, computational abilities, and various technologies, IoT devices can communicate and exchange data across the internet or other networks. This field merges elements of electronics, communication, and computer science engineering. It involves a network of interconnected devices, emphasizing the technology that facilitates their communication, such as cloud-based platforms. Common household items, like light bulbs, cameras, and TVs, are transformed into active participants of the Internet ecosystem by connecting to this network.

IIoT: The Industrial Internet of Things (IIoT) enhances and broadens the scope of the Internet of Things (IoT) across various professional environments and practical applications. It prioritizes inter-machine connectivity, helping sectors and enterprises elevate their operational efficiency and dependability. Among its chief uses are robotics, medical apparatus, and production processes governed by software.

ICS: Industrial Control Systems (ICS) are integral to operations in sectors such as manufacturing and the distribution of energy and materials. These systems vary in complexity from straightforward single-panel controllers to elaborate setups encompassing extensive distributed control systems with several field connections. They leverage a range of technologies, with SCADA systems, programmable logic controllers (PLC), and distributed control systems (DCS) being particularly prominent.

IACS: Industrial Automation and Control Systems (IACS) are essential parts of most critical infrastructures and critical services. IACS refers to all the components (PLCs, SCADA, HMI, etc.) integrated into essential infrastructures and industrial production establishments.

OT, ICS, & SCADA Security: The above diagram shows clear and distinct boundaries for IT, OT and IoT. However, the picture is changing with the advancement of technology. OT security has become essential. In the past, OT and ICS (Industrial Control Systems) were kept separate from other systems.

They were not connected to the internet. Everything in these systems was controlled locally, directly through control panels, and they worked in a self-contained environment. However, as technology has advanced, these industrial devices are now being connected to the internet as a part of digital transformation, the emergence of Industry 4.0 ecosystem, data analytics, predictive maintenance, etc. This change is part of a larger digital transformation in the industry. There's a convergence between IT (Information Technology) and OT, along with connections to cloud-based services.

This IT & OT convergence means that the traditional air gap that existed in IT and OT devices is vanishing. Industrial devices, which were mainly made to be safe, reliable, and productive, are now facing new challenges. When these devices were designed, they mainly focused on operating safely and efficiently. Cybersecurity was not a major concern at that time because these devices were not connected to broader networks or the internet. Now, with these devices being online for monitoring and other purposes, it's crucial to have strong OT security. Being connected to the internet makes them vulnerable to cyber threats and attacks. If these systems are compromised, it could lead to serious problems, not just in terms of data security but also in terms of physical safety and operational productivity. Therefore, ensuring the cybersecurity of these systems is essential to protect them from potential threats that come with internet connectivity.

1.7 THE DIFFERENCE BETWEEN IT AND OT

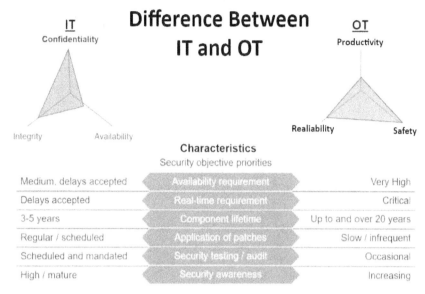

Characteristics		
	Security objective priorities	
Medium, delays accepted	Availability requirement	Very High
Delays accepted	Real-time requirement	Critical
3-5 years	Component lifetime	Up to and over 20 years
Regular / scheduled	Application of patches	Slow / infrequent
Scheduled and mandated	Security testing / audit	Occasional
High / mature	Security awareness	Increasing

Information Technology (IT) and Operational Technology (OT) differ fundamentally in their objectives and the environments they operate within. Information Technology (IT) is traditionally focused on data and the secure management of information, using the CIA triad: Confidentiality, Integrity, and Availability. This means IT systems prioritize keeping data private (confidentiality), ensuring it is accurate and unaltered (integrity), and making sure it is accessible when needed (availability).

On the other hand, OT primarily ensures physical processes' Safety, Reliability, and Availability, SRA Triad. In the OT world, safety is paramount because OT systems interact with real-world physical devices. For example, in an industrial setting, if an OT system fails, it could lead to machinery malfunctioning, potentially causing injury or even death. Therefore, OT systems are designed with a stronger emphasis on preventing physical accidents and ensuring that the systems are always running (availability).

In the IT world, some downtime is often acceptable. For instance, if an online service is down for a few hours in a year, it's generally not a critical issue. However, in OT, such as with a metro train system, even a small amount of downtime can have severe consequences, like trains derailing or not stopping at the stations as scheduled. The requirement for real-time performance is also more intense in OT. Delays of even milliseconds in sending and receiving signals can lead to significant issues, such as misalignment of metro train doors or improper mixing of chemicals in a treatment plant, which could have disastrous outcomes.

OT devices like PLCs and RTUs are expected to operate continuously for many years without updates, making cybersecurity challenging. Patching vulnerabilities and conducting security testing are slow and infrequent processes in OT environments. Additionally, cybersecurity awareness among OT personnel working on-site is generally lower than among average IT professionals.

1.8 COMPONENTS OF OPERATIONAL TECHNOLOGY:

Operational Technology (OT) and Industrial Control Systems (ICS) are terms often spoken of interchangeably, yet they denote distinct concepts within the industrial tech landscape. ICS specifically relates to the elements of technology dedicated to process control, employing systems such as SCADA—which allows for supervisory control and data acquisition and integrating devices like human-machine interfaces (HMI) or programmable logic controllers (PLCs).

On the other hand, OT encompasses a broader range of technologies that include but are not limited to, control mechanisms. This includes software embedded within operational equipment or utilized for overarching management and monitoring functions. Delineating these categories is fundamental for a comprehensive mastery of the OT ecosystem, pivotal for both strategic oversight and the bolstering of industrial defenses.

Visual aids often clarify such distinctions; consider examining the diagram below, which maps out the relationship and hierarchy between OT and ICS within the operational framework.

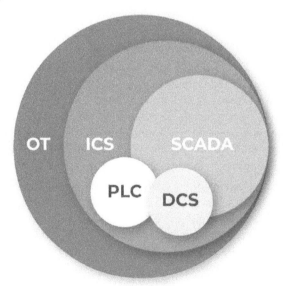

Operation technology Security:

OT security revolves around implementing protective measures and controls to shield operational technology (OT) systems from cybersecurity risks. These systems are responsible for automating and overseeing industrial processes that rely on specialized software.

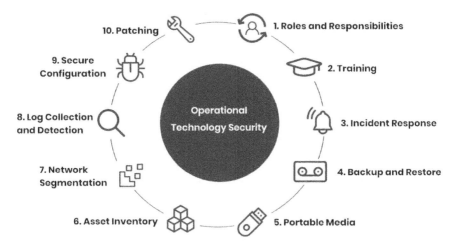

The increasing convergence of information technology (IT) and OT has amplified the demand for robust OT security. Before IT/OT convergence, OT systems were isolated and inaccessible to online threats. However, IT/OT integration has brought about greater automation but has exposed them to cyberattacks such as malware and ransomware. These OT assets are now integral parts of complex networks, adding to their susceptibility to threats. The diversity of OT systems, including industrial control systems (ICS) like supervisory control and data acquisition (SCADA) and distributed control systems (DCS), further complicates security efforts. Breaches can result in catastrophic consequences, including operational disruptions, physical damage, and risks to the safety of personnel and the environment.

OT security encompasses a range of technologies and practices aimed at safeguarding assets, data, and the management of physical OT devices and processes. This includes deploying various security technologies like next-generation firewalls, Security Information and Event Management systems (SIEM), and access control measures. Despite the niceties brought about by the convergence of IT and OT networks, achieving effective OT security is feasible through comprehensive visibility across the attack surface and the implementation of tailored security policies to meet the unique requirements of the OT environment. The ultimate objective of OT security is to protect critical processes, people, and profitability while minimising vulnerabilities and security incidents.

SCADA Security:

SCADA systems, standing for Supervisory Control and Data Acquisition, are pivotal in managing and overseeing complex operations across various industries. These systems centralize data collection from sensors and devices, allowing operators to control processes remotely. Their implementation spans multiple sectors, including manufacturing, energy, water management, and transportation, enhancing efficiency, ensuring safety, and reducing operational downtimes. SCADA's ability to deliver real-time insights significantly aids in decision-making and facilitates process automation to refine industrial operations.

However, the security of these SCADA systems presents several challenges:

- **Legacy Systems:** Initially designed in eras prior to the establishment of contemporary cybersecurity norms, many SCADA frameworks are prone to security vulnerabilities.

- **Increased Connectivity:** As SCADA systems become more interconnected with external networks, including the Internet, they face elevated risks of cyberattacks, broadening their exposure.

- **Authentication Flaws:** Older systems often lack robust authentication protocols, which can lead to unauthorized access to critical infrastructures.

- **Encryption Gaps:** Weak encryption practices may leave the data transmissions within SCADA systems susceptible to interception and manipulation. Neglecting to install timely updates and security patches can leave systems open to exploits by known threats.

The implications of a compromised SCADA system are severe, ranging from operational disruptions to significant financial losses, not to mention the potential safety risks that could affect essential services like water, electricity, and transportation. The importance of securing SCADA systems extends beyond data protection—it is critical for maintaining continuous service delivery and ensuring the safety of operators.

In response to these vulnerabilities, a robust security framework for SCADA systems is essential. This framework should encompass governance, risk assessment, compliance with regulatory standards, and tailored security measures for data protection. It is designed to fortify defenses against evolving cyber threats while maintaining system functionality and process fidelity. Additionally, third-party entities involved in the development and maintenance of SCADA systems must comply with strict security regulations to enhance overall security measures.

Industrial Control System (ICS) Security:

ICS security is all about safeguarding industrial control systems, encompassing hardware and software that oversee and manage operations. These systems are integral to the functioning of critical infrastructure such as power plants and manufacturing facilities. The security measures in place aim to protect these complex systems from cyber threats, ensuring data integrity, machinery safety, and uninterrupted operations. The essence of ICS security lies in safeguarding both the systems and networks tightly intertwined with industrial processes. The security here is not solely digital; it extends to ensuring the physical safety of the operational environment.

As these systems become increasingly interconnected with broader IT ecosystems, the demand for robust security protocols has grown. Each component within ICS, including Programmable Logic Controllers (PLCs) and Human-Machine Interfaces (HMIs), requires specific security measures to mitigate the risks of unauthorized access, data breaches, and system malfunctions. A breach in ICS security doesn't just jeopardize data integrity but can disrupt industrial processes, resulting in operational downtime, financial losses, and, in extreme cases, threats to human safety. The existing defense mechanisms and cybersecurity solutions are designed to be both proactive and responsive. This approach involves identifying and mitigating potential threats before they impact the system while also having responsive measures in place to contain and neutralize threats that breach initial security defenses.

1.9 DIFFERENCE BETWEEN IT AND OT SECURITY:

Information Technology (IT) Security and Operational Technology (OT) Security represent two distinct sectors within the field of cybersecurity, each targeting specific objectives and employing different strategies.

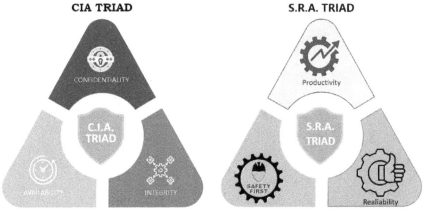

Information Technology   Operational Technology

- **Objectives:** IT Security is primarily focused on the protection of data through the principles of confidentiality, integrity, and availability, often abbreviated as the CIA Triad. It also ensures adherence to various regulatory standards such as GDPR, HIPPA, and PCI-DSS. OT Security, on the other hand, prioritizes safeguarding against physical threats and environmental impacts, emphasizing the reliability and consistent availability of industrial operations, encapsulated by the acronym SRA (Security, Reliability, Availability).

- **Areas of Concentration:** The domain of IT Security encompasses the safeguarding of digital financial and personal data, computer systems, network infrastructure, and digital assets. Conversely, OT Security is dedicated to the protection of physical processes, industrial control systems (ICS), and essential infrastructure elements.

- **Technological Deployment:** In IT, the technology utilized includes widely available commercial IT hardware and software, such as laptops and servers. OT employs specialized, often custom-built, technology designed for longevity and tailored to specific industrial functions.

- **Network Connectivity:** IT environments typically feature devices connected through modern networks using ethernet, Wi-Fi, or fibre optics. Although OT systems have traditionally operated within isolated or air-gapped networks, there is a growing trend towards greater connectivity with IT networks, enhancing integration but also introducing new vulnerabilities.

- **Update and Patch Management:** Within IT environments, security updates and patches are regularly implemented to address vulnerabilities. In contrast, OT environments tend to apply updates less frequently. The emphasis on uninterrupted system availability often leads to a more cautious approach to patching, which might be delayed to prevent disruption of operational processes.

1.10 CURRENT ISSUES WITH OT/ICS SECURITY

Current challenges in operational technology (OT) and industrial control systems (ICS) security are increasingly complex and multifaceted, reflecting the dynamic nature of cyber threats and specific obstacles associated with these environments.

Enhanced Risk Through IIoT Adoption: The swift incorporation of Industrial Internet of Things (IIoT) devices within OT infrastructures is escalating security risks. While these devices promote operational efficacy, they simultaneously broaden the potential avenues for cyber-attacks, intensifying the susceptibility of OT systems. The intricacy and interconnectedness of these networks complicate their security and management.

Impact of Hacktivism and Global Political Tensions: Politically motivated cyber activism, or hacktivism, is evolving in sophistication and destructiveness, particularly within OT settings. Such attacks not only disrupt operations but can also result in substantial physical damage to the systems involved. This trend is expected to intensify as international political tensions increasingly dictate cyber warfare tactics.

Prevalence of Ransomware and Financially Driven Attacks: Ransomware continues to be a significant threat within OT environments, targeting vital infrastructure for monetary benefits. These assaults can disrupt operations directly and have broader effects on supply chains and economic stability.

Difficulties in System Maintenance: Regular updates and patches are challenging to implement in many OT systems due to their critical operational roles and the necessity for constant uptime. This leaves systems exposed to potential exploits, particularly when they rely on outdated software or when existing vulnerabilities remain unaddressed for extended periods.

Security Concerns with Open-Source Software in OT: The use of open-source software within OT frameworks is raising security concerns. Efficiently managing these software components, addressing vulnerabilities in a timely manner, and securing the software supply chain are essential but challenging tasks that require coordinated efforts across the industry.

Physical Repercussions of Cyber Incidents: The tangible effects of cyber incidents on OT systems are increasingly pronounced, leading to operational halts and significant shutdowns. This highlights the urgent need for enhanced cyber defense measures capable of preventing or reducing the impact of such incidents.

Strategies and Considerations:

Addressing the security concerns in Operational Technology (OT) and Industrial Control Systems (ICS) demands a specialized strategy due to their unique challenges. Here are essential strategies and considerations:

Educational Programs and Protocol Standardization:

- **Specialized Training for Proprietary Protocols:** Initiate training programs tailored for IT professionals on the specific protocols utilized by leading companies, such as Siemens. Collaborate with these corporations to broaden training resources and opportunities.

- **Advocacy for Universal Standards**: Champion the adoption of universal protocols throughout the industry to reduce security risks linked to proprietary systems and streamline security operations.

Enhanced Patch Management Processes:

- **Custom Patch Management Strategies:** Forge patch management solutions that respect the unique demands of updating ICS/OT systems, potentially aligning patch deployment with scheduled maintenance to reduce system downtime.

- **Consistent Vulnerability Assessments:** Set up regular scanning and evaluation protocols to identify and rectify vulnerabilities promptly.

Advanced Encryption Practices:

- **Tailored Encryption Solutions:** Investigate and apply encryption technologies that accommodate the restricted processing capabilities of OT systems. Consider lightweight cryptographic approaches for efficiency.

- **Secure Data Transmissions:** Prioritize the encryption of data in transit within ICS environments, employing specialized solutions designed for these systems' specific limitations.

Robust Defense Mechanisms:

- **Layered Security Approaches:** Implement a multi-layered security framework that includes comprehensive security measures, network segmentation, and periodic system evaluations.

- **Advanced Intrusion Detection Systems (IDS):** Utilize sophisticated IDS to monitor network traffic within ICS settings and identify patterns indicative of cyber threats or anomalies.

Resilience and Rapid Recovery Capabilities:

- **Enhanced System Resilience:** Incorporate redundancy within systems to ensure that failures or security breaches in one component do not compromise overall network integrity.

- **Proactive Incident Response Plans:** Develop incident response strategies that emphasize quick isolation of compromised systems to mitigate damage and contain security breaches.

Compliance with Regulations and Adoption of Best Practices:

- **Regulatory Compliance:** Ensure adherence to industry-specific regulations and standards set by bodies such as the International Society of Automation (ISA) or the National Institute of Standards and Technology (NIST).

- **Ongoing Audits and Updates:** Regularly review and refine security protocols to align with evolving cyber threats and technological advancements.

PURDUE MODEL

2.1 INTRODUCTION: PURDUE MODEL

The Purdue Model was originally developed to streamline information management in computer-integrated manufacturing, where computers oversee the entire production process to enhance speed and reliability. Over the years, it evolved into a standard framework for constructing network systems in Industrial Control Systems (ICS), bolstering Operational Technology (OT) security by segmenting the network into distinct layers. This segmentation facilitates orderly data flow between layers, creating a protective barrier or "air gap" between ICS/OT systems and conventional IT systems. Such isolation enables organizations to implement stringent security measures without disrupting their routine operations. The resilience of industrial operations is crucial as it directly influences a company's revenue and customer well-being when OT networks operate seamlessly. A cyber-attack on industrial environments can render systems inoperable, significantly affecting core operations. Even a brief loss of visibility for operators monitoring network activities can necessitate a shutdown due to concerns over product quality and safety. Disruptions in physical processes can lead to decreased productivity, financial losses, and, in severe cases, pose risks to human safety.

Government alerts frequently highlight methods used by adversaries to penetrate organizations. These methods include spear-phishing to breach IT networks and subsequently accessing the OT network, directly connecting to internet-exposed controllers without requiring user or device authentication, and exploiting known vulnerabilities in IT and OT devices and software. Once inside, malicious activities can persist undetected for extended periods due to the often-limited security measures in place on OT networks. This emphasizes the critical need to enhance security in operational technology to safeguard against potential threats and vulnerabilities.

Purdue Model: The Purdue Model is predicated on the concept of separation between IT and industrial infrastructure to keep the OT crown jewels devices and components disconnected from and inaccessible to the IT network and the internet.

The Purdue Enterprise Reference Architecture is based upon the commonly used architectural reference model authored in the 1990s for control systems. The Purdue model provided a framework for segmenting industrial control system networks from corporate enterprise networks and the Internet. The model is used as a baseline architecture for all industrial control system frameworks, such as API 1164 and NIST 800-82. The diagram below shows the Purdue model, various levels and different industrial components of each layer.

Levels of Purdue Model:

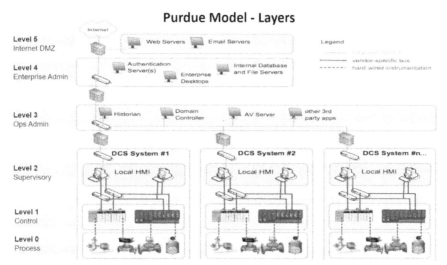

The Purdue Model provides an approach, to comprehending the framework of Industrial Control Systems (ICS). It categorizes the system into five levels, with each level elaborated upon in the following sections provided below:

2.2 LEVEL 0: FIELD DEVICES AND PROCESSES

Description: Level 0 serves as the foundational layer in the Purdue Model, essential for comprehending industrial systems. At this stage, we encounter the physical processes and equipment forming an industrial setup. This layer encompasses various devices like sensors, actuators, valves, pumps, and more. These devices directly interact with and oversee real-world processes within the industrial environment.

Function: At Level 0, field devices are pivotal in data collection from industrial processes. These devices gather information such as temperature, pressure, flow rates, and other parameters from real-world operations. They also have the ability to execute commands to control these physical processes, making necessary adjustments to ensure smooth and efficient operation within the industrial system.

Significance: Level 0 is crucial for the control and monitoring of industrial processes. This is where real-time action occurs, with data collected directly from the physical world. This data is then transmitted to higher-level control layers for analysis and decision-making. Level 0 is the starting point in the chain of information flow within the industrial system, ensuring that data from physical processes is available for further assessment and control at higher levels.

Level 0
Process

Devices: Sensor / Actuators / Transmitters / Robots / Motor Drives

Devices: Level 0 includes devices that do not perform any information processing. Common devices in industrial processes are:

1. **Sensors:** These devices collect data from the physical environment, such as temperature, pressure, flow rates, and levels. Examples include temperature sensors, pressure transducers, and flow meters.

2. **Actuators:** Actuators execute actions based on control signals received from higher-level systems. Examples include motorized valves, pumps, and motors.

3. **Switches:** Switches control simple on/off operations in the process. They include limit switches, push-button switches, and proximity sensors.

4. **Instrumentation Devices:** Instruments like analyzers, pH meters, and conductivity sensors provide specific measurements crucial for process control and monitoring.

5. **Safety Systems:** Safety-related devices such as emergency shutdown systems (ESD) and safety instrumented systems (SIS) protect personnel and assets in case of emergencies.

Additionally, Level 0 may include other machinery responsible for assembly, lubrication, and other physical processes.

2.3 LEVEL 1: PROCESS CONTROL

Description: The process control layer, situated just above Level 0 in the Purdue Model, leverages data from Level 0 sensors to oversee and manage specific industrial processes or units. This stage is crucial for ensuring these processes run smoothly and adhere to desired specifications. By receiving data from Level 0 sensors, it issues commands to Level 0 actuators to make necessary adjustments, keeping process parameters within set limits, thus enhancing operational efficiency.

Function: At this stage, control systems utilize data from field devices and employ predefined algorithms to make informed decisions. These decisions are crucial for maintaining the stability and efficiency of industrial operations.

Essentially, this level functions as the operational brain, analyzing data and taking actions to ensure everything runs effectively and without interruptions.

Significance: The primary responsibility of Level 1 is to ensure the optimal functioning of individual processes within an industrial facility. Key objectives include maintaining safety, quality, and efficiency. Additionally, Level 1 plays a pivotal role in optimizing processes, enhancing their effectiveness and efficiency.

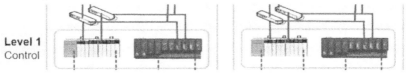

Devices - PLCs / RTUs / PACs / I-O Module

Devices:

Level 1 encompasses essential "Basic Control" devices, such as:

1. **Programmable Logic Controllers (PLCs):** PLCs are fundamental for local control and automation tasks. They receive input from sensors and execute control logic to regulate processes, making them indispensable at this level.

2. **Remote Terminal Units (RTUs):** RTUs are crucial in industries like utilities and oil and gas for monitoring and controlling remote equipment and processes. They gather data from sensors and relay it to higher-level systems.

3. **Programmable Automation Controllers (PACs):** These controllers are versatile, capable of incorporating higher-level instructions, and are used in various automation tasks.

4. **I/O (Input/Output) Modules:** These modules link PLCs and DCS to field devices like sensors and actuators, facilitating data exchange between the control system and the field.

2.4 LEVEL 2: SUPERVISORY CONTROL

Description: Elevating from the foundational elements set at Level 1, the Area Supervisory Control layer manages multiple process control units within a designated segment of an industrial facility. This tier is pivotal in coordinating and supervising Level 1 systems to assure seamless and effective operations within the area.

Functions: This layer consolidates data from Level 1 controllers and serves as a central observation point, monitoring the health and performance of processes in a particular area. It is tasked with the implementation of complex control strategies that elevate the functionality of linked units, effectively bridging the granular control at Level 1 with the broader optimization objectives of the plant.

Significance: The importance of Level 2 lies in its ability to enhance coordination and operational efficiency within a distinct area of the industrial facility. It ensures that processes are aligned smoothly, preventing potential conflicts and inefficiencies that could emerge from the interactions among multiple Level 1 controllers. Essentially, this layer acts as a facilitator to maintain orderly operations within its designated zone.

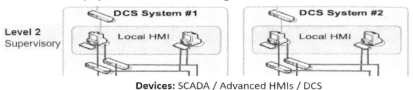

Devices: SCADA / Advanced HMIs / DCS

Devices:

Often referred to as the "Supervisory Control" level in the Purdue Model, Level 2 employs the following key devices:

1. **SCADA Systems:** These systems are integral at Level 2 for their advanced control and monitoring capabilities, supervising a range of PLCs, RTUs, and other field devices.

2. **Advanced Human-Machine Interfaces (HMI):** At this level, HMIs are equipped to provide detailed insights about the entire operation, supporting real-time monitoring, data logging, and extensive reporting capabilities.

3. **Distributed Control Systems (DCS):** These systems offer centralized control and monitoring for multiple PLCs and field devices, furnishing a unified interface for operators to oversee various aspects of the operation.

4. **Remote Monitoring and Control:** These systems enable remote access and control over industrial processes, allowing operators to adjust and oversee operations from remote locations.

5. **Alarm Management Systems:** Responsible for the creation and management of alerts during abnormal conditions, these systems assist operators in quickly responding to potential issues.

2.5 LEVEL 3: SITE SUPERVISORY CONTROL

Description: Level 3 extends its reach across an entire industrial setting, managing various sectors, units, and operations. This tier functions as the primary supervisory layer, tasked with the integration and orchestration of processes throughout the facility. Therefore, Level 3 ensures that diverse operational segments, units, and procedures are seamlessly and efficiently interlinked across the industrial environment.

Functions: In this layer, pivotal decisions are made concerning resource distribution, energy management, and the overall operational efficacy of the site. Level 3 provides an exhaustive viewpoint of the facility, enabling strategic allocation and maximization of resources. Fundamentally, this level adopts a comprehensive approach to ensure optimal and effective site operations.

Significance: The importance of Level 3 stems from its key role in enhancing the overall output of the industrial site. Its main objective is to synchronize all operations and areas to meet the strategic and business goals of the company collectively. Essentially, Level 3 functions as the central coordinator, ensuring all components of the industrial site are aligned to achieve the company's objectives efficiently.

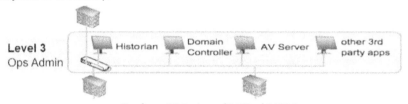

Devices: Historians / MESs / MOMs

Devices:

Regarding technology, Level 3 within the Purdue Model encompasses systems aimed at supervising and refining manufacturing operations. Essential devices and systems in this layer include:

1. **Historian Systems:** These are critical for the storage and archival of historical operational data collected from lower-tier devices. This data is essential for in-depth analysis, troubleshooting, and maintaining compliance with regulations.

2. **Manufacturing Execution Systems (MES):** At Level 3, MES software is crucial. It facilitates the management of manufacturing operations by tracking work orders, scheduling production, monitoring equipment performance, and compiling data for analytical and reporting purposes.

3. **Manufacturing Operations Management (MOM):** This encompasses a set of systems designed to oversee the complete manufacturing process, focusing on enhancing efficiency. MOM software includes various applications such as production management, performance evaluation, and compliance and quality control.

This layer represents the upper boundary of the Operational Technology (OT) layer. All devices at this level and below are considered OT devices.

2.6 LEVEL 4: ENTERPRISE BUSINESS PLANNING

Description: Situated at the top of the Purdue Model, Level 4 transcends the immediate operational focus of the preceding layers. It establishes the crucial nexus between Industrial Control Systems (ICS) and higher-order enterprise systems such as Enterprise Resource Planning (ERP) and other business management platforms. This tier is pivotal in merging industrial functions with broader corporate roles, enabling fluid interaction and synchronization between the tactical operations and strategic dimensions of a company.

Functions: The primary function of Level 4 centers on strategic planning and high-level decision-making, with a keen alignment of ICS with overarching corporate ambitions. This level is tasked with resource allocation, the formulation of production timelines, and the execution of market analyses. Its fundamental purpose is to synchronize day-to-day industrial activities with the wider business objectives, fostering a unified and progressive operational framework.

Significance: The critical responsibility of Level 4 is to align the operations within the Industrial Control Systems with the global strategic blueprint of the organization. Serving as the conduit between granular operational choices at the lower tiers and the expansive corporate targets, this level ensures the alignment of routine ICS operations with the company's long-term strategic aims.

Devices: Business Planning and Logistics

Devices: Known as the 'Business Planning and Logistics' tier within the Purdue Model, Level 4 encompasses the systems and components that orchestrate business operations and their integration into the manufacturing sphere."

2.7 LEVEL 5 DMZ LAYER

The Purdue Model includes a specific layer known as the Demilitarized Zone (DMZ), which is strategically placed between the Operational Technology (OT) components, reaching up to level 3, and the Information Technology (IT) systems at level 4 and beyond. To secure this crucial DMZ zone, firewalls are extensively utilized.

Key infrastructure elements housed within the DMZ include Patch Management Servers, Intrusion Detection/Prevention Systems (IDS/IPS), Jump Servers, and Historians. These devices are essential for both the security and operational efficacy of the OT environment.

The fundamental role of the DMZ is to manage and control interactions between the OT and IT realms, adding an extra layer of security that protects the OT domain. This setup acts as a defensive shield, preventing unauthorized access and potential threats that could compromise essential OT systems and disrupt industrial operations.

Level 5
Internet DMZ

Devices: Public facing web services

Devices:

For devices positioned at Level 3.5 in the Purdue Model—an optional but often implemented level—several critical systems are typically incorporated within the DMZ for enhanced protection:

- **Anti-Virus Server**: This server tackles significant threats and malicious software by regularly updating its virus definitions from the internet and distributing these to endpoints in lower layers to bolster security.

- **Patch Server**: Similar to the Anti-Virus Server, the Patch Server is tasked with acquiring security updates and software patches from the internet. It is pivotal in maintaining the currency and security of devices at lower levels.

- **Remote Access Server**: Positioned within the OT layer, this server facilitates remote management of specific devices like PLCs and sensors through secure vendor operations, ensuring both safety and efficiency in device handling.

03 OT SECURITY AS PER NIST SP 800-82 REV 3

3.1 INTRODUCTION: NIST SP 800-82 REV 3 GUIDELINES, A FRAMEWORK FOR OT SECURITY

The 'Guide to Industrial Control Systems (ICS) Security,' also known as NIST SP 800-82 Rev 3, is an essential framework published by the National Institute of Standards and Technology (NIST) aimed at bolstering cybersecurity measures within Operational Technology (OT) systems. These systems include but are not limited to those used in manufacturing, power generation, and water treatment facilities, integral to managing and controlling physical operations and processes.

Distinguished from traditional IT environments, OT systems present unique challenges including the necessity for continuous operations, stringent real-time data processing, and extended lifecycles of the equipment. To address these, NIST SP 800-82 Rev 3 outlines specific objectives:

1. **Security Protocols**: The guide delineates extensive security practices tailored to the operational context of OT systems. These include creating robust risk management frameworks, formulating specific security policies, and establishing proactive incident response strategies.

2. **Architectural and Network Safeguards**: It underlines the criticality of implementing secure network architectures, advocating for the integration of firewalls, demilitarized zones (DMZs), and virtual private networks (VPNs). These measures help segregate OT networks from broader corporate networks and the internet, thus mitigating potential cyber threats.

3. **Component Defense Mechanisms**: Recommendations extend to securing the individual components of OT systems, such as sensors, actuators, and controllers. This involves strengthening authentication, authorization, and auditing functions to ensure system access is strictly controlled and monitored.

4. **Vulnerability Oversight**: The document advises routine vulnerability assessments to pinpoint and address security weaknesses. It promotes patch management strategies that align with the operational continuity of the systems.

5. **Incident Management and Recovery**: Special emphasis is placed on crafting incident response plans that consider the operational and safety aspects of the OT environments. Effective communication strategies and swift recovery protocols are advised to minimize operational disruptions and expedite system restoration to normalcy.

6. **Governance and Regulatory Compliance**: The guideline also highlights the role of governance in sustaining security, urging organizations to integrate cybersecurity into their corporate governance structures to make security a persistent element of operational strategy.

Challenges in Implementation: Despite the clear advantages, adopting these guidelines can be complex, particularly for organizations operating older systems that may not support current security protocols, coupled with the need for specialized knowledge to manage OT security effectively.

Educational Value: For students and professionals specializing in cybersecurity with a focus on industrial settings, this document provides valuable practical knowledge that connects theoretical cybersecurity principles with the practical demands of safeguarding critical infrastructure.

In essence, NIST SP 800-82 Rev 3 serves as a crucial guide for both seasoned professionals and learners, offering structured methods to enhance the security of industrial control systems and ensure the continued safe and efficient operation of essential services."

NIST Cybersecurity Framework:

The NIST Cybersecurity Framework offers a method for managing cybersecurity risks in organizations. Let us break down the elements to grasp their significance and functionality:

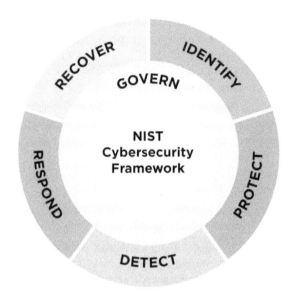

Identify: This initial stage focuses on understanding the organizations systems, assets, data and potential risks. It is crucial to recognize what requires protection and the possible business impacts if these assets are compromised. Tasks include managing assets, governance and assessing risks.

Protect: Once vulnerabilities are identified the next step involves implementing measures to protect these assets. This includes setting up safeguards to ensure the delivery of essential services. Protection measures may involve access control, data security strategies, regular security protocol maintenance and utilizing technologies for resilience.

Detect: The Detection component aims at identifying cybersecurity incidents. Early detection is crucial for facilitating a response. This entails monitoring and employing detection processes to ensure awareness of any unusual activities.

Respond: Having a defined response plan is vital in case of a cybersecurity incident. This function outlines the steps for addressing detected incidents, such as communicating with stakeholders, analyzing incidents, mitigating damage to prevent harm and making enhancements for future responses.

Recover: After an incident, it is crucial to get things on track by fixing any disruptions in services or capabilities. The recovery process aims to return to operations, lessening the impact of the incident. This includes planning for recovery, making necessary enhancements and communicating steps to restore systems and business functions.

At the heart of the framework lies governance emphasizing oversight and risk management strategies. It stresses the importance of evaluations and revisions to keep up with the changing cybersecurity threats and maintain compliance with policies and regulations.

3.2 SCADA SYSTEMS

Supervisory Control and Data Acquisition (SCADA) systems are vital for monitoring and regulating industrial operations across several industries. These industries span from water distribution to public transit, and all rely on the effective administration of distributed assets. SCADA systems offer centralized control and monitoring, resulting in a unified picture of an operation's numerous inputs and outputs. This brief review seeks to educate SCADA systems by highlighting their components, functions, and usefulness in industrial processes.

Core Components of SCADA Systems

SCADA systems are made up of both hardware and software components that work together to guarantee that industrial operations run smoothly and can be controlled from a single place. The important components are:

- **Control Servers:** Serve as the primary hub for processing data and executing commands.
- **Engineering Workstations:** Used to build and test system setups.
- **Historians:** Databases that save all process data for future examination.
- **Human-Machine Interface (HMI):** Displays process data to operators in real-time.
- **RTUs and PLCs:** Remote Terminal Units RTUs and Programmable Logic Controllers PLCs communicate with field equipment to gather data and execute commands.
- **Communication Equipment:** Enables data transfer between the control center and the field stations.
- **Sub Control Servers:** Manage communication loads in huge networks to maximize efficiency.

Comprehensive Layout of SCADA Implementation

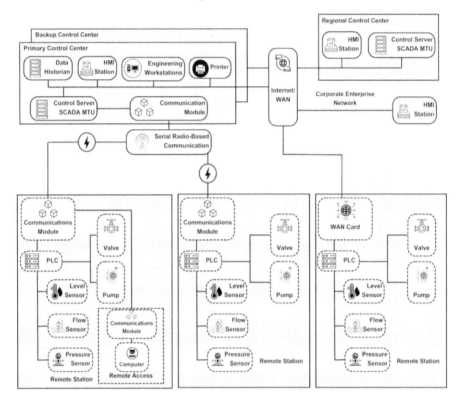

Functionality of SCADA Systems

At its center, SCADA systems collect data from numerous field stations and send it to a centralized control center. The HMI allows operators to monitor and control the process using visual or textual representations. Depending on their setup and the demands of the industry they serve, these systems can run automatically or with user input.

Communication & Control

SCADA systems use a variety of communication methods and topologies to connect control centers with distant field stations. These might include cable connections, wireless communications such as radio telemetry, and internet-based approaches. Communication topologies are created depending on the geographical distribution of components and the system's specialized requirements, ranging from point-to-point to more sophisticated networks.

Cybersecurity and Redundancy

Given the vital nature of the processes that SCADA systems regulate, cybersecurity and fault tolerance are essential. Redundancy is integrated into crucial components of systems to make them more secure. However, because these devices frequently communicate over public networks, they are vulnerable to cybersecurity risks and require strong technological restrictions.

A complete SCADA structure generally consists of a primary control center, field locations, and perhaps a backup control center for redundancy. Communication between these components can take several forms, with some using radio telemetry and others using WAN. A regional control center may provide an extra layer of supervisory control above the major control center, with access to the corporate network for remote troubleshooting and maintenance.

SCADA systems are essential for the effective functioning of many industrial sectors, providing centralized monitoring and control over distributed equipment. Understanding the components and performance of these systems is critical for anybody attempting to comprehend the complex nature of current industrial processes. Their contribution to the continuity and dependability of essential infrastructures cannot be emphasized, emphasizing the need for cybersecurity measures to protect these crucial systems.

3.3 DISTRIBUTED CONTROL SYSTEMS (DCS)

Distributed Control Systems (DCS) are integral frameworks that govern manufacturing operations across various regions and industries. This segment delves into the concept of DCS, detailing its functionality, structure, and significance in enhancing industrial efficiency and reliability.

Utilization of DCS Across Industries

DCS systems are pivotal in managing intricate manufacturing processes across diverse sectors due to their supervisory capabilities. Notable industries utilizing DCS include:

- Water treatment and management.
- Production of electrical power.
- Exploration and processing in the oil and gas sector.
- Refinery operations.
- Automated production lines.
- Pharmaceutical production.

These systems are crucial for the seamless and efficient operation of production activities within these sectors.

Distributed Control System

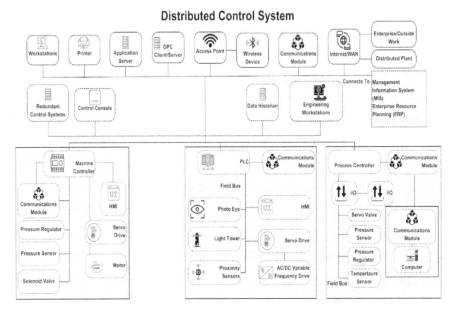

Fundamental Elements of DCS

A DCS is characterized by several key components that collectively ensure control over production processes:

- **Central Supervisory Control:** This component oversees the entire operation, ensuring cohesive functioning of all subsystems.

- **Localized Controllers:** These are responsible for managing specific segments of the manufacturing process, thus ensuring detailed control.

- **Communication Networks:** Facilitate communication between the central supervisory control and localized controllers.

- **Modular Structure:** Enhances the resilience of the system by minimizing the impact of any malfunctions.

Key Features and Benefits

- **Integrated Control:** DCS systems provide a holistic approach to managing complex production systems, which includes both an overarching supervision and targeted local control.

- **Resilience:** The modular nature of DCS systems ensures that malfunctions in one module minimally impact overall operations, thus enabling quick identification and rectification.

- **Industry-Specific Protocols:** DCS systems employ established communication protocols such as Modbus, Fieldbus, Profinet, TCP/IP, and OPC to ensure seamless operation and integration.

Significance of DCS in Industrial Settings

DCS systems are essential for enterprises that require precise control over multiple manufacturing processes within the same vicinity. By compartmentalizing production systems, DCS enhances operational efficiency and minimizes downtime caused by system failures. Additionally, DCS systems can be integrated with enterprise networks to provide insights into business operations and support decision-making through role-based access controls.

In conclusion, Distributed Control Systems are crucial for modern industrial operations, offering robust and efficient management and monitoring of production processes. Their ability to compartmentalize and mitigate the effects of system failures, along with their use of standardized communication protocols, establishes DCS as a fundamental tool in the automation and control of complex industrial activities.

3.4 PROGRAMMABLE LOGIC CONTROLLER-BASED TOPOLOGIES

Programmable Logic Controllers (PLCs) are specialized computer systems crucial for automating and managing industrial operations. These controllers are integral to numerous operational technologies, particularly within SCADA (Supervisory Control and Data Acquisition) systems and DCS (Distributed Control Systems). This section aims to provide insights into the functionalities and unique advantages of PLCs in these environments.

The Functionality of PLCs in SCADA and DCS Environments

PLCs are central to the operations of both SCADA and DCS as they manage specific segments of industrial processes. Their usage is consistently critical across these systems:

- **In SCADA Systems:** PLCs gather data from field devices and execute commands to control processes at the local level.

- **Within DCS Environments:** PLCs function within a hierarchical control structure, performing tasks directed by a superior control system like the Siemens Power and Process Automation SPPA-T3000.

Principal Components and Characteristics

Known for their robustness and versatility, PLCs are designed to withstand diverse industrial environments with minimal human intervention. Their main characteristics include:

- **User-Programmable Memory:** This feature allows the storage of instructions for executing diverse functions such as logic operations, timing, counting, PID control, arithmetic tasks, and handling data.

- **Autonomous Operational Control:** PLCs can independently run pre-set tasks indefinitely, ideal for operations requiring consistent or static logic.

- **System Flexibility:** In smaller operational technology systems, PLCs can serve as the primary controllers, managing specific processes directly.

Programmable Logic Controller (PLC)

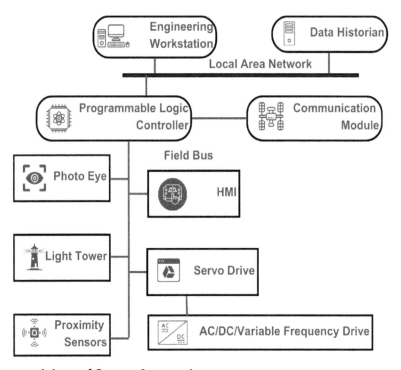

Connectivity and System Integration

PLCs are engineered for seamless integration with various components of industrial control systems:

- **Engineering Workstations:** These provide a user interface for PLC programming, configuration, and management.

- **Data Historians:** Essential for archiving operational data for future analysis and reporting.

- **Local Area Networks (LAN):** Facilitate the communication between PLCs and other system components like workstations, enhancing the coordination and efficiency of process control.

Programmable Logic Controllers are indispensable in contemporary industrial scenarios, offering precision control, flexibility, and reliability. Gaining a basic understanding of PLC operations within SCADA and DCS frameworks is crucial for anyone interested in the scope and functionality of operational technology.

3.5 BUILDING AUTOMATION SYSTEMS

Building Automation Systems (BAS) are specifically designed operational technology (OT) systems that manage and control multiple procedures within a structure. These systems are critical in managing heating, ventilation, air conditioning (HVAC), fire safety, electrical systems, lighting, and security to keep the building environment comfortable, safe, and energy efficient. This section introduces BAS explaining its significance, components, and benefits for modern infrastructure.

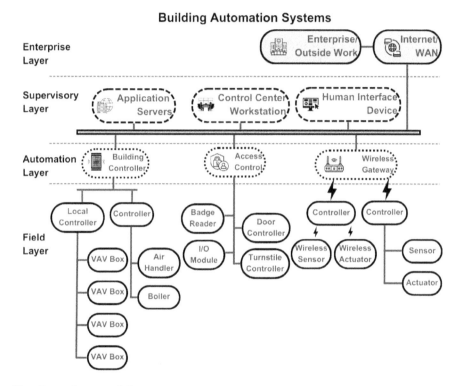

Key Functions and Components

BAS pairs a variety of procedures and technology to produce a comprehensive building management system. The major functions are:

- **Heating, Ventilation, and Air conditioning (HVAC):** Provides the best indoor air quality and thermal comfort.

- **Fire Safety Systems:** Detect and respond to fire dangers to safeguard persons and property.

- **Electrical and Lighting Control**: Controls lighting systems to improve efficiency and convenience.

- **Security Systems:** Includes access control and monitoring to safeguard the safety of inhabitants.

Building Automation System components are typically similar to Distributed Control Systems (DCS), with distributed parts communicating with central controllers or gateways over wired or wireless networks.

Examples include:

- **Environmental Control Sensors:** Monitor temperature and humidity and change settings as needed.
- **Variable Air Volume (VAV) Boxes:** Regulate airflow in response to controller inputs to maintain desired environmental conditions.
- **Access Control System:** Verify the occupant's credentials before granting or denying admission.

Benefits of Building Automation Systems:

The use of BAS in contemporary structures has various advantages:

- **Energy Efficiency:** Improves the usage of heating, lighting, and air conditioning to save energy.
- **Cost Savings:** Reduces operating and maintenance expenses through effective system management.
- **Improved Comfort and Safety:** Maintains ideal conditions and strengthens security measures to ensure occupant comfort and safety.
- **Improves Building Security:** Achieved by integrating access control and surveillance systems.

Retrofitting and Modernization

While newer buildings are frequently constructed with BAS from the start, older ones might benefit from retrofitting. Retrofitting involves modifying equipment and systems to allow for the integration of automation technology, which extends the benefits of BAS to older buildings.

Building automation systems are an essential component of modern building management, providing considerable increases in energy efficiency, operating cost savings, and occupant comfort and safety. Understanding the components and functions of BAS allows readers to comprehend the value these systems provide to new and renovated buildings.

3.6 PHYSICAL ACCESS CONTROL SYSTEMS

Physical Access Control Systems (PACS) are critical security systems that limit admission into certain locations or facilities, ensuring that only authorized personnel have access. These systems play an important role in ensuring the security and integrity of an organization's premises by controlling and monitoring access rights. This topic is intended to provide a basic overview of PACS, its components, and how they work to protect facilities from unauthorized access.

Physical Access Control Systems

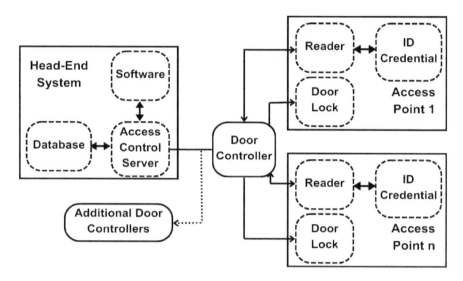

Key Components of PACS

PACS functioning is based on several important components, each of which plays a distinct role in the access control process:

Access points are physical obstacles where access control is used, such as doors, turnstiles, and vehicular gates.

- **Identification Credentials:** Devices or information used to identify a person requesting access, including, passwords, key fobs, key cards, encrypted badges, or mobile credentials.

- **Readers and keypads:** Devices installed at entry points to read information from identifying credentials.

- **Door Controllers:** Hardware that accepts credential data from readers and determines whether access is given.

- **Access Control Server:** A central system that saves user information, and access rights, and keeps an audit trail of all access attempts.

The Access Control Process

The procedure of regulating access using PACS consists of multiple steps:

- **Credential Presentation**: Authorized users provide their identifying credentials at the access point.

- **Credential Verification:** The reader or keypad collects credential information and delivers it to the door controller, who then sends it to the access control server for validation.
- **Access Decision:** If the access control server verifies and approves the credentials, the control panel unlocks the door and allows admission. If the credentials are refused, the door will stay locked.
- **Logging:** The door controller logs all access attempts, whether successful or refused, and stores them in the access control server for audit reasons.

Enhanced Security Measures

To increase security, PACS may employ two-factor authentication, which requires users to submit a second form of verification (such as a PIN or biometric scan) after giving their primary credentials. This increases security by combining something the user has (such as a key card) with something the user knows (a PIN) or is (a biometric feature).

PACS Server and Data Management

The Access Control Server is an essential component of PACS, serving as a store for user data, access privileges, and audit logs. This server can be hosted on-premises or maintained in the cloud, depending on the organization's requirements and the specific PACS deployment.

Physical access control systems are critical for protecting sensitive areas and ensuring that only authorized workers have access to certain portions of a building. Understanding the components and processes of PACS allows readers to realize the complicated procedures involved in ensuring safe and regulated access to buildings and facilities.

3.7 SAFETY SYSTEMS

Safety systems are crucial within the industrial realm, serving as protectors of human life, assets, and environmental integrity. These systems are specifically engineered to mitigate risks associated with operational technology (OT) systems that manage physical operations, potentially leading to hazardous conditions. The focus of this discussion is to elucidate the concept, elements, and significance of safety systems in an industrial setting in a manner that is both comprehensible and engaging.

Basics of Safety Systems

Safety systems are designed to substantially decrease the probability and impact of hazardous events by ensuring the safe termination of processes. Distinct from ordinary malfunction-induced shutdowns, safety systems guarantee that facilities transition to a secure state both smoothly and effectively. They form a vital part of a plant's comprehensive risk mitigation framework, tailored to align with the organization's tolerance for risk.

Key components include:

- **Emergency Shutdown (ESD) Systems:** These systems are activated to halt operations swiftly in the event of an emergency, preventing harm.

- **Process Safety Shutdown (PSA) Systems:** These systems are triggered to perform shutdowns when specific process hazards are detected.

- **Fire and Gas Systems (FGS):** These systems are crucial for detecting and addressing fire and gas leaks, helping avert catastrophic outcomes.

- **Safety Instrumented Systems (SIS):** These are specialized for executing designated safety functions upon detecting particular conditions.

Safety Instrumented Systems

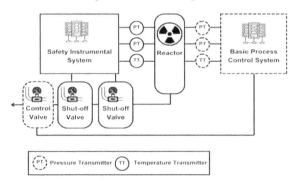

Traits of Industrial Safety Systems

Industrial safety systems are marked by several attributes that bolster their reliability and efficiency:

- **Enhanced Redundancy:** This feature ensures the system remains operational and effective even if individual components fail.

- **Safety Integrity Level (SIL) Certification:** Not every control system meets the rigorous requirements for SIL certification, which quantifies the risk reduction provided by a safety function.

- **Independent Operation:** Safety Instrumented Systems (SIS) are typically configured to operate independently from other control systems, preventing failures in the basic process control systems (BPCS) from affecting the SIS.

Implementing Safety Systems

The application of safety measures in industrial environments is tailored to the specific needs and recognized hazards of each facility. Some systems are:

- **Standalone Safety Systems:** These are designed to be both physically and logically separate from other control systems to ensure seamless safety operations.

- **Integrated Control and Safety Systems (ICSS):** These systems facilitate interactions between the SIS and other control systems such as DCS for monitoring, logic processing, and data logging purposes.

Cybersecurity Measures

As the integration of IT and OT environments advances, securing the cybersecurity of safety systems becomes imperative. Strategies include:

- **Application-Level Firewalls:** These manage data flow to and from safety systems, permitting only authorized interactions.
- **Role-Based Access Control (RBAC):** This restricts access to the system based on an individual's role within the organization, ensuring only authorized personnel have entry.
- **Application Whitelisting:** This allo
- ws only pre-approved applications to operate, minimizing the risk of malicious software intrusions.

Industrial safety systems are indispensable for maintaining the operational integrity, security, and safety of facilities. By integrating advanced technologies with stringent safety protocols, these systems help prevent accidents and protect lives and property, underscoring their essential role in modern industrial operations. Understanding the components, functionality, and importance of these systems underscores the vital need for industrial safety.

3.8 INDUSTRIAL INTERNET OF THINGS

The Internet of Things (IoT) revolutionizes communication among objects and humans, bringing automation and data exchange to diverse sectors such as manufacturing, home automation, and healthcare. This concept is structured around three key levels: the edge, platform, and enterprise tiers, each critical to the IoT network.

Industrial Internet of Things

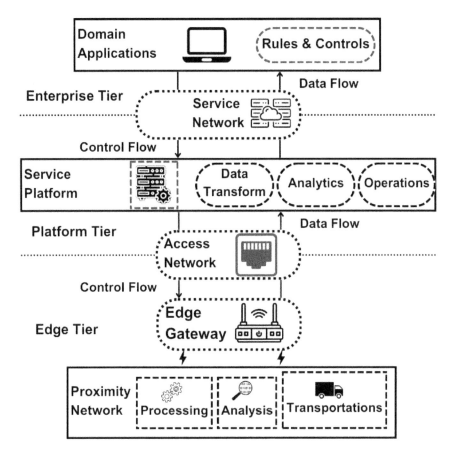

Exploring the Three Tiers of IoT:

1. Edge Tier This tier marks the initial point of contact with devices and sensors gathering environmental data. It's characterized by its varied geographic and operational environments, utilizing both stationary and mobile devices. Notable elements include:

- **Edge Nodes:** These are the devices, like sensors and actuators, responsible for collecting and transmitting data.

- **Proximity Network:** This network links edge nodes to broader IoT infrastructure through gateways, facilitating connection to larger networks.

2. Platform Tier Acting as the intermediary layer, the platform tier manages data translation, analytics, and the dispatch of commands. It bridges the lower edge and upper enterprise tiers, processing incoming data and executing directives based on complex algorithms. Key functions are:

- **Data Processing and Analytics:** This involves analyzing edge data and formatting it for higher-level use.

- **Access Network:** It provides necessary connectivity for data and control flows between the edge and platform tiers, utilizing various communication methods like private networks and cellular connections.

3. Enterprise Tier Positioned at the top, the enterprise tier encompasses domain-specific applications and decision-support tools. It offers an interface for end-users to interact with the IoT system, enabling them to send commands and monitor operations. Components include:

- **Domain-Specific Applications:** These are tailored applications that adapt functionalities to suit different IoT uses.

- **Service Network:** This network secures the connection between the platform services and enterprise applications, facilitating data and command exchanges.

Key IoT Concepts:

- **Edge Computing:** This concept refers to distributed computing resources along the data path from sources to the cloud. It allows for real-time data processing and actions directly at the data source.

- **Distributed Interactions:** IoT supports varied interaction models, including peer-to-peer and device collaboration, enabling devices to perform complex tasks or work together to enhance operations independently.

IoT Communication Networks:

The structure relies on three principal networks:

- **Proximity Network:** Connects edge devices to nearby gateways.

- **Access Network:** Links edge gateways to platform services.

- **Service Network:** Bridges platform services with enterprise applications, ensuring secure data flow.

The Internet of Things integrates intelligence and connectivity into a vast array of devices. Understanding its three-tier structure and the role of edge computing helps grasp the extensive capabilities and potential of IoT to transform industries and everyday activities. This overview serves as a basis for exploring how IoT can drive innovation, operational efficiency, and enhanced decision-making across various sectors.

04 OPERATIONAL TECHNOLOGY CYBERSECURITY PROGRAM

4.1 INTRODUCTION: OT CYBERSECURITY PROGRAM

This chapter explores the establishment and execution of a detailed Operational Technology (OT) Cybersecurity Program, influenced by the guidelines set forth by the National Institute of Standards and Technology (NIST). It discusses critical procedures and considerations for formulating, revising, and preserving a strong cybersecurity framework that is designed to shield crucial OT systems, such as those found in manufacturing sectors and utility services. The significance of this program is highlighted by its crucial role in defending these infrastructures against cyber threats, promoting operational reliability, and facilitating adherence to changing regulatory demands. With comprehensive instructions on crafting the program, managing risks, and seamlessly integrating with IT security measures, this section offers indispensable insights for students keen on mastering and deploying effective cybersecurity strategies in practical OT settings.

4.2 OT CYBERSECURITY PROGRAM DEVELOPMENT

Operational Technology (OT) systems are key components of many industries, regulating anything from manufacturing to utility services. As these devices link to the internet and integrate with IT networks, the significance of an effective OT cybersecurity program grows. This section describes the necessary processes and considerations for building or revising an OT cybersecurity program under the National Institute of Standards and Technology (NIST) recommendations.

Priority	Category
1	Program Creation
2	Regular Updates
3	Comprehensive Approach
4	Risk Management

1. Program Creation and Development

The key component of a secure OT environment is the development or modification of a cybersecurity program that includes particular measures designed to safeguard OT systems such as Distributed Control Systems (DCS) and Programmable Logic Controllers (PLCs). The program should:

- **Roadmap Development:** Create a clear roadmap outlining the actions and efforts that will be implemented over a certain period to improve OT cybersecurity.

- **IT Security Alignment:** Ensure that the OT cybersecurity measures are consistent with existing IT security policies to avoid and mitigate cyber risks that may cross between IT and OT systems.

- **Unique Needs Assessment:** Address the unique needs of OT systems, which may differ greatly from standard IT settings.

2. Regular updates and adaptations

An evolving approach to cybersecurity needs frequent revisions to the cybersecurity program to account for new systems, technologies, and regulatory requirements. This includes:

- **Technology Integration:** Implementing security concerns and checks for new systems and technologies that are being implemented.

- **Regulatory Compliance:** Updating the program in response to new cybersecurity legislation and requirements to ensure continued compliance.

3. Comprehensive Approach

Creating a complete cybersecurity program requires establishing specific objectives, scopes, policies, and processes. It requires:

- **Policy and Procedure Documentation:** All cybersecurity policies and procedures should be clearly documented and shared throughout the organization.

- **Cross-Functional Team Formation:** Assemble a team with various skills, including IT, cybersecurity, OT equipment, and process control systems. The combination of disciplines provides a comprehensive picture of cybersecurity threats and solutions.

4. Risk Management

The cybersecurity program prioritizes identifying and managing cyber hazards. Effective risk management includes:

- **Risk Prioritization:** Use tools like the Common Vulnerability Scoring System (CVSS) or vulnerability priority ratings to evaluate and prioritize risks based on their potential effect.

- **Continuous Monitoring:** Use continual monitoring and evaluation procedures to detect new risks and vulnerabilities as they arise.

The creation and maintenance of an OT cybersecurity program is a continuous process that involves careful planning, frequent updates, and a complete risk management strategy. Organizations may better defend themselves against the ever-changing world of cyber threats by integrating OT security measures with larger IT security standards and addressing the special demands of operational systems. Following the NIST recommendations offers a solid foundation for creating a cybersecurity program that protects important operational technology while also assuring the stability and safety of essential services.

4.3 ESTABLISH CHARTER FOR OT CYBERSECURITY PROGRAM

In the world of operational technology (OT), implementing an effective cybersecurity program is key to protecting critical infrastructures and ensuring the continuity of essential services. Creating a charter for the OT cybersecurity program is an important first step in the process. This section explains the relevance of a charter, its components, and how it fits into the larger organizational cybersecurity framework, with an emphasis on accessibility.

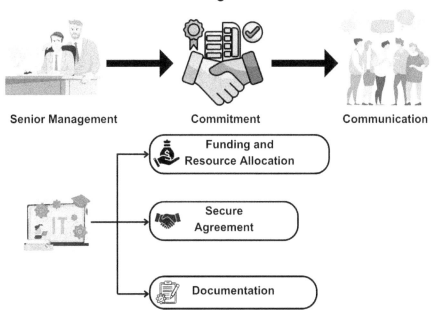

Purpose of the Charter

A charter serves as an official expression of top management's commitment to cybersecurity throughout the organization. It is a top-down strategy that shows leadership's commitment to protecting OT systems against cyber-attacks. The charter serves many vital functions:

- **Establishes Authority:** Specifies that the cybersecurity program is supported by top management, giving it essential authority and credibility.

- **Defines Leadership:** Leadership is defined as appointing a cybersecurity manager to lead the efforts, ensuring that the program has clear leadership and direction.

Aspects of the Charter

A carefully planned charter for an OT cybersecurity program comprises many key elements:

- **Program Objectives:** Describes the goals and scope of the cybersecurity initiatives, including what the program wants to accomplish.

- **Roles and Responsibilities:** Plans the duties of the cybersecurity manager and other important staff, creating clear ownership and accountability for securing OT resources.

Integration with Organizational Cybersecurity: Highlights that the OT cybersecurity program should not be run in isolation, but rather as part of the organization's overall cybersecurity strategy.

Benefits of Integration:

Integrating the OT cybersecurity charter with the organization's overall cybersecurity program provides various benefits.

- **Resource Efficiency:** Allows for the exchange of resources, such as people, technology, and information, making cybersecurity projects more efficient and cost-effective.

- **Alignment with Business Goals:** Makes certain that cybersecurity measures are in line with the organization's purpose and business objectives, highlighting the relevance and value of cybersecurity activities.

- **Leveraging Existing Practices:** Uses current cybersecurity practices inside the organization, customizing them to fit the particular demands of OT systems while ensuring consistency in cybersecurity methods across the board.

Developing a charter for an OT cybersecurity program is an important first step toward developing a complete cybersecurity posture that protects essential operational systems. The charter establishes the foundations for successful cybersecurity governance by proving senior management's commitment, assigning clear leadership, and guaranteeing integration with the whole organizational cybersecurity architecture. This dedication not only improves the security of OT systems but also strengthens the general endurance and dependability of the organization's operations.

4.4 BENEFITS OF THE OT CYBERSECURITY PROGRAM

Upon obtaining acceptance for the OT cybersecurity program's business case, it is critical to communicate the benefits of investing in cybersecurity measures. According to National Institute of Standards and Technology (NIST) rules, these benefits apply to a wide range of operational technology systems, including safety, dependability, and efficiency. This section focuses on the reasoning and implications of cybersecurity investments, to make the argument plain and understandable.

Benefits of Cybersecurity Investments:

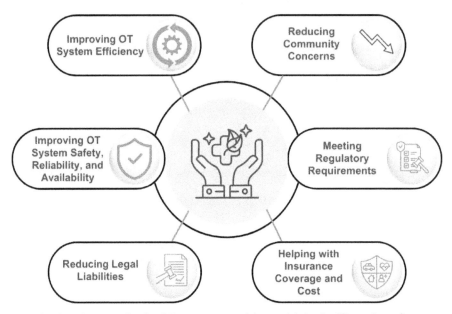

Benefits of Cyber Security Investments

Investing in cybersecurity for OT systems provides multiple significant benefits, each of which contributes to the overall improvement of operations and risk management:

- **Improved Safety and Reliability:** Improves the safety, dependability, and availability of OT systems by protecting against potential cyber-attacks that might compromise system performance.

- **Increased Efficiency:** By identifying and correcting non-performing assets and possible bottlenecks in the network, cybersecurity solutions may greatly increase system performance.

- **Governance and Process Acceleration:** Implementing governance mechanisms, such as job assignments, improves procedures and speeds up operational activities.

- **Community Trust:** Demonstrates a commitment to system and data security, hence reducing community concerns.

- **Legal and regulatory compliance**: Assists organizations in meeting regulatory obligations, therefore lowering the risk of legal action.

- **Financial Benefits:** Showcasing strong cybersecurity safeguards will help you get greater insurance coverage and perhaps cut your insurance expenses.

Impacts of Cyber Attacks

Impacts of Cyber Attacks

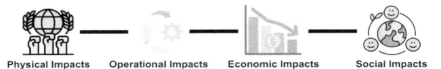

Physical Impacts   Operational Impacts   Economic Impacts   Social Impacts

Cyber incidents on OT systems can have far-reaching implications, ranging from immediate operational interruptions to physical, economic, and societal dimensions:

- **Physical Impact:** This refers to the possibility of bodily damage or loss of life, highlighting the crucial necessity for strict cybersecurity measures.

- **Operational Impact:** This can impact the operations system, leading complete loss of production for a number of days. Loss of control or view of a critical system in a plant.

- **Economic Impact:** Cyber incidents may result in large financial losses, including direct revenue loss, manufacturing downtime, and downstream economic impacts throughout the supply chain and market.

- **Social Impact:** The reputational harm caused by a cyber assault may reduce public trust in an organization, lowering its status and trustworthiness on a national or even worldwide scale.

The motivation for investing in OT cybersecurity is comprehensive, addressing not just the immediate improvement of system safety and efficiency, but also the mitigation of larger economic and societal concerns. Organizations may better appreciate the importance of implementing strong cybersecurity measures by presenting the overall advantages of cybersecurity investments as well as the possible consequences of cyber-attacks. Following NIST standards, organizations may create a convincing case for OT cybersecurity activities, highlighting the value of such investments in protecting operational technology systems against a continually evolving threat landscape.

4.5 OT CYBERSECURITY PROGRAM CONTENT

An efficient Operational Technology (OT) cybersecurity program is extensive, comprising several categories vital to securing critical infrastructure from cyber-attacks. This section describes the key components of an OT cybersecurity program, highlighting accuracy and availability.

OT Cybersecurity Content

1. Program Setup

A well-structured configuration adapted to the specific needs of each OT environment serves as an essential component of a strong OT cybersecurity strategy. This includes:

- **Asset-Specific Considerations:** Creating the program to account for each equipment or work unit across several OT locations.
- **Inter-Team Coordination:** Enabling efficient coordination across Industrial Control Systems ICS, Information Technology IT, process control, and automation teams for effectively coordinated security efforts.

2. Policy Exceptions

Identifying and managing exceptions to cybersecurity standards is critical for:

- **Handling Deviations:** Developing methods for when it is not possible to completely comply with the intended regulations, ensuring flexibility without affecting security.

3. Risk Management

Risk management is a critical component of any cybersecurity program and includes:

- **Assessment and Response:** Performing risk assessments to identify vulnerabilities and choosing the right response acceptance, transfer, mitigation, or avoidance.

4. Legacy Systems Security

To address the security demands of legacy systems, which may lack vendor support, requires:

- **Tailored Security Measures:** Using specific security solutions, such as improved firewalls or increased border protection, to defend these older systems.

5. Understanding Priorities

Understanding the basic changes in objectives between IT and OT security is critical.

- **Priority Shift:** In contrast to IT, where secrecy is crucial, OT security values system uptime to ensure uninterrupted operations.

6. OT Governance and Coordination

Appropriate OT governance and coordination provides a framework for handling cybersecurity responsibilities:

- **Role Definition and Access Control:** Clearly stating who maintains certain systems, the degree of access provided, and the cybersecurity duties.
- **Legal and Risk Management:** Determining that those in authority are fully educated about cybersecurity rules and their legal and risk consequences.

An OT cybersecurity program covers a wide range of topics, including program creation and inter-team cooperation, as well as risk management and OT governance. Important stages include adjusting cybersecurity measures to meet the specific demands of new and old systems, understanding the unique objectives of OT settings, and creating effective governance. This extensive approach not only protects OT systems from possible cyber-attacks but also integrates cybersecurity activities with the organization's overall goals, therefore improving the reliability and safety of critical operational technology.

4.6 CYBERSECURITY PROGRAM IMPLEMENTATION TEAM

To establish a cybersecurity program for Operational Technology (OT) it is essential to collaborate across departments within an organization. This section covers the formation of a cybersecurity team, their responsibilities and the importance of their training in safeguarding the security and resilience of OT environments.

OT Cyber Security Program Team

Form the Team

Share Knowledge

Resource Model

Security Design

Roles & Responsibilities

Integration with IT

Funding and Expectation

Continuous Improvement

1. Team Formation

The step in implementing a comprehensive OT cybersecurity initiative is assembling a cross-disciplinary team comprising;

- **IT Experts:** Focused on integrating security measures into OT systems.
- **Control Engineers and System Operators**: Addressing the operational requirements and constraints of control systems.
- **Security Engineers and Risk Management Specialists:** Handling specific security challenges and risk factors relevant to OT environments.
- **Cybersecurity Service Providers:** Offering expertise and support, for implementing cybersecurity solutions.
- **Safety Advisors:** Ensuring that cybersecurity measures uphold industrial safety standards without compromising reliability.

2. Knowledge Sharing

To ensure the effectiveness of the cybersecurity program, it is necessary to:

- **Encourage Knowledge Exchange:** Team members should share their fields of expertise and experience so that they can address and manage OT cybersecurity threats together.
- **Define Roles and Responsibilities:** Define specific roles for the creation, operation, and advancement of the cybersecurity program, including those of third-party suppliers.

3. Resource Modelling

Deciding on the organization of the cybersecurity team involves:

- **Choosing the Right Resource Model**: Deciding whether to recruit personnel, engage contractors, or outsource responsibilities to a managed security service, taking into account considerations such as location, money, and organizational requirements.

4. Design for Security

The collaboration between control system engineers and IT departments is critical for:

- **Developing a Security Design:** Using the team's combined expertise to design a security architecture that assures the integrity and availability of OT systems.

5. Role and Responsibilities

To ensure the effectiveness of the cybersecurity program, it is necessary to:

- **Define Roles and Responsibilities:** Define specific roles for the creation, operation, and advancement of the cybersecurity program, including those of third-party suppliers.

6. Integration with IT.

Instead of functioning in isolation, the OT cybersecurity program should be:

- **Integrated with IT Security:** Confirm that OT cybersecurity management is consistent with IT cybersecurity and corporate risk management standards.

7. Funding and Expectations Alignment

Securing acceptable money and having realistic goals is critical for:

- **Aligning Expectations and Resources:** Working with management to establish risk tolerance, residual risk, and security objectives within the limits of available resources.

8. Continuous Improvement.

A successful cybersecurity program involves continuous review and improvement:

- **Implementing Continuous Improvement:** The cybersecurity program is regularly updated and refined to handle changing threats and integrate best practices.

The formation and training of an OT cybersecurity program team are essential for the security and efficiency of operational technology environments. Organizations may build effective cybersecurity measures adapted to their unique needs by creating a diverse team, encouraging information exchange, and establishing clear roles and responsibilities. Integrating these efforts with IT security, matching expectations with available resources, and committing to ongoing improvement are all critical steps toward protecting OT systems from cyber threats.

4.7 OT CYBERSECURITY STRATEGY

Implementing an operational technology (OT) cybersecurity plan is an important step for organizations trying to protect their most crucial infrastructure from cyber-attacks. Considering the National Institute of Standards and Technology (NIST) recommendations, this section describes an organized strategy for establishing an extensive OT cybersecurity plan that addresses the unique demands of OT settings.

OT Cyber Security Strategy

| Foundation | Leverage Existing | Refinement | Team Identification |
| Architecture | Training | Risk Tolerance | IT/OT Concerns |

1. Foundation: Organizational Risk Management

The foundation of a successful OT cybersecurity strategy is based on an organization-wide risk management framework. This basic phase includes:

- **Identifying Core Risks:** Recognizing the organization's major risk elements that may affect OT operations.

- **Risk management Inputs:** Using these findings to create the cybersecurity strategy for OT systems.

2. Leverage Existing Frameworks

Enhancing existing resources and frameworks is critical for efficiency:

- **Integrating current Infrastructure:** Using current risk assessments, tolerance levels, and threat models to reduce redundancy.

- **Tailoring for OT:** Making these components relevant to the OT cybersecurity scenario.

3. Refinement:

Addressing OT Constraints. Modifying the method to address the particular problems of OT systems necessitates that:

- **Protocol and Legacy System Considerations:** Adjusting the method to accommodate unique operational restrictions, such as protocol limits and legacy system integration.

4. Team Identification

Creating a focused cybersecurity team is essential for plan implementation.

- **Resource Allocation:** Choosing whether to use existing workers, hire new employees, or contract for external expertise.
- **Role Definition:** Assigning particular cybersecurity roles and duties within the organization.

5. Architectural Outline

Creating an extensive cybersecurity architecture is crucial for protection.

- **Systematic Planning:** Creating a cybersecurity architecture that includes several locations and OT systems across the organization.

6. Training and Awareness

Developing skills and awareness within the organization comprises:

- **Regular Training:** Providing both general cybersecurity awareness programs and particular training for skill improvement.

7. Risk Tolerance

Improving how the organization views and manages risk in OT operations.

- **Setting Priorities:** Setting priorities based on the criticality ratings of OT assets and adjusting risk management actions accordingly.

8. Addressing IT/OT Concerns

Understanding the unique issues of the IT and operational environments.

- **IT Concerns:** Include data loss, system availability, and data breaches.
- **OT Concerns:** Focuses on system safety, manufacturing efficiency, and environmental preservation.

Designing an OT cybersecurity plan based on NIST recommendations offers a complete approach to protecting vital operational technology. Organizations may build a strong cybersecurity posture by creating a solid foundation of organizational risk management, using existing frameworks, and refining the approach to satisfy OT-specific demands. Critical stages include identifying a dedicated team, selecting an acceptable operating model, establishing cybersecurity architecture, and prioritizing training and risk tolerance. Further, understanding the specific issues of IT and OT will allow organizations to create a risk-mitigation plan that supports operational efficiency and safety.

RISK MANAGEMENT FOR OT SYSTEMS

5.1 INTRODUCTION: RISK MANAGEMENT FOR OT SYSTEMS

This chapter focuses on the methods, for handling security vulnerabilities in Operational Technology (OT) settings. It outlines an approach for recognizing, assessing, alleviating and overseeing risks in OT systems for maintaining the reliability and operational effectiveness of key infrastructures. Structured around risk management principles this section offers insights into using established risk management frameworks, those endorsed by the National Institute of Standards and Technology (NIST). Understanding these ideas is crucial for students as it equips them to safeguard services and infrastructure from evolving cybersecurity threats ensuring operational dependability and security.

5.2 MANAGING OT SECURITY RISK

OT security risk management is crucial, for safeguarding infrastructure and upholding the availability of services. It involves identifying and mitigating risks in a changing environment where threats and vulnerabilities persistently evolve. This topic delves into the elements of overseeing OT security risks.

Key Components of Risk Management

Four Key Activities

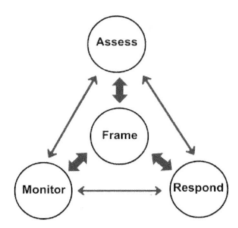

The management of OT security risks can be broken down into four interconnected components:

- **Frame:** The initial step in risk management involves creating a framework for decision-making. This establishes guidelines on what needs protection and why.

- **Assess:** This phase evaluates threats and vulnerabilities, determining the existence of risks their impact on operations and their probability.

- **Respond:** In response to the risk assessment this component entails taking action to mitigate identified risks, such as implementing security measures and protocols.

- **Monitor:** Consistently monitoring and reporting on the risk landscape is crucial. This ongoing process ensures detection and addressing of emerging risks.

Continuous Iteration

Risk management, in OT, is a process that adapts to evolving risks, vulnerabilities and organizational procedures. It emphasizes the importance of monitoring and adjusting security protocols to adapt to the evolving environments.

Types of Risks

Securing OT involves assessing types of threats such as:

- **Cybersecurity Threats:** Concerns related to cyberattacks and data breaches.

- **Physical Threats:** Dangers stemming from access to OT systems and devices.

- **Safety Concerns:** hazards that could lead to harm or fatalities.
- **Financial Risks:** The impacts of security incidents and risk management strategies.

Management Levels

Appropriate OT security risk management works at three levels within an organization:

- **Organization Level:** This top-level viewpoint offers the overall context and direction for risk management, incorporating senior management and an advisory board.
- **Mission/Business Process Level:** This mid-level focuses on controlling risks unique to certain missions or business processes, as directed by the organizational level.
- **System Level:** The most detailed level, closer to operational systems and procedures. It is concerned with applying risk management measures directly on OT systems and reporting up the management structure.

Comprehensive Security Approach

A thought-out plan ensures that risk management goals and tasks are aligned across all levels of the company. This detailed strategy encourages transparency making it easier to track decisions and share information effectively throughout the organization. Two-way communication is essential, enabling information to flow downward and ensuring that all parts of the organization are well-informed and synchronized in their security measures.

Effectively managing technology (OT) security risks necessitates an approach involving ongoing risk assessment, planning, response and supervision. By implementing a tiered management strategy encompassing the entire company, businesses can gain a comprehensive understanding of their risk landscape. This proactive and thorough approach is crucial, for safeguarding OT environments against threats while upholding reliability and safety standards.

5.3 FRAMING OT RISK

Understanding and addressing security threats in Operational Technology (OT) serves as essential for protecting critical infrastructures. This procedure takes an organized approach to identifying, assessing, and mitigating possible dangers. Based on the National Institute of Standards and Technology (NIST) suggestions, we go into the main parts of structuring OT security risk, to make it accessible and helpful.

Continuous and Interconnected Processes

Risk management in OT is a dynamic, continuing activity that necessitates constant review and change to meet the changing risk picture. It is not sequential; monitoring can change the framing, and fresh evaluations can result in updated responses.

Key Considerations in Framing Risk

Framing OT Risk

Personnel Safety

Availability

Interconnectedness

Risk Assessment

Important factors to consider when framing risks are defined below:

- **Personnel Safety:** Prioritize safety to protect people and property from danger, taking into account both physical and digital threats.

- **Legacy Systems:** Evaluate the specific vulnerabilities of legacy systems that may not support current cybersecurity solutions.

- **Availability:** Plan system substitutes to ensure continuous operation, particularly for critical infrastructures with significant interdependence.

- **Interconnectedness:** Identify and manage the risks associated with the linked nature of OT systems across industries and activities.

OT Impact Level Assessment

Financial loss, safety hazards, environmental damage, and reputational injury are among the factors to consider when assessing the effect of future security events. Frameworks such as the National Institute of Standards and Technology (NIST) Federal Information Processing Standards (FIPS) NIST FIPS 199, and International Society of Automation (ISA) and International Electrotechnical Commission ISA/IEC 62443 can be used to classify and prioritize risks based on their potential impact on confidentiality, integrity, and availability.

Understanding Likelihood

Understanding the likelihood of cybersecurity occurrences is critical for consistent risk assessment, which includes threat information, historical data, security measure efficacy, and active Advanced Persistent Threats (APTs).

Using Heatmaps for Risk Analysis

Heatmaps are a visual tool in the risk analysis process that helps to demonstrate the likelihood of threats exploiting vulnerabilities and the possible severity of their effect.

Framing OT security risk requires a complete strategy that includes understanding the underlying context, using existing technologies, fine-tuning methods to fulfill OT-specific demands, and regularly monitoring and updating risk management processes. Organizations can establish successful OT environment protection policies by taking into account safety, system availability, interconnection, and the consequences of possible security events. Using standards and tools like NIST guidelines and heatmaps, as well as considering the likelihood of attacks, allows organizations to prioritize activities and spend resources more efficiently, assuring vital operational technologies' resilience and security.

5.4 ASSESSING RISK

Understanding and mitigating security threats in operational technology (OT) is key to ensuring the integrity, safety, and efficiency of critical infrastructure operations. This section presents an organized plan for measuring OT security risk using the concepts specified in several standards such as National Institute of Standards and Technology NIST, International Electrotechnical Commission IEC 62443, and International Organization for Standardization ISO 27001.

Risk Assessment Process

| Initiation | Objective | Levels | Cross-Level |

Initiation of Risk Assessment

The risk assessment process starts with:

- **Use of Predefined Methodologies:** Applying established frameworks for risk assessment, including management techniques and specified tolerance boundaries.

Defining objectives

Clear objectives are required for successful risk assessment:

- **Identifying, Estimating, and Ranking Risks:** Highlighting the importance of operations that may be compromised.

Organizational Levels of Risk Assessment

A complete risk assessment includes three main levels:

- **Organization Level:** Provides an overall background for risk management, with top management guiding the strategic direction.
- **Mission and Business Process Level:** Focuses on risks to specific missions or business processes, guided by organizational-level instructions.
- **System-Specific Level:** Risks are targeted at the system level, with a focus on direct impacts on operational technology devices and processes.

Cross-level Utility

Information gathered at one level should feed risk assessments at other levels, ensuring a thorough awareness of risk throughout the organization.

Key Components of Risk Assessment

The risk evaluation comprises the following:

- **Identification:** Involves identifying risks and weaknesses.
- **Analysis:** Involves determining the probable consequences of identified threats and vulnerabilities.
- **Likelihood Estimation:** Calculating the likelihood of undesirable outcomes caused by recognized threats and vulnerabilities.

Dual Impact Consideration

Physical and Digital Impacts: Understanding that cybersecurity events can have both physical (equipment damage) and digital (data theft) effects.

Key Considerations

Important factors to consider while assessing risks include:

- **Regular Updates:** Maintaining risk assessments following the changing operating environment.
- **Vulnerability Identification:** Involves using resources such as advisories and national vulnerability databases to discover possible problems.
- **Environmental Considerations:** Incorporate the influence of environmental conditions on OT systems into the risk assessment.
- **Physical Asset and Security Controls:** Assessing physical security measures' performance in safeguarding OT assets.
- **Business Continuity Planning:** Involves developing rapid response methods to protect operations in the event of a security compromise.
- **Control Mechanism Review:** Evaluates both digital and mechanical controls in place to effectively limit risks.

Assessing OT security risk requires an organized approach that includes a starting point, objective setting, extensive analysis at all organizational levels, and consideration of dual implications. Organizations may gain a more in-depth understanding of their risk environment by concentrating on detection, analysis, and likelihood estimation. Regular updates, environmental concerns, physical security measures, business continuity planning, and control mechanism assessments all improve the security posture. This organized strategy guarantees resilience to possible attacks, protecting the continuity and integrity of vital operating technology.

5.5 RESPONDING TO RISK

Addressing security concerns in Operational Technology (OT) requires a systematic and strategic strategy to ensure key system resilience and safety. A set of established actions can assist organizations in efficiently navigating the difficulties of OT security. The procedure is divided into simple, achievable sections to give a complete guide.

Responding to Risk

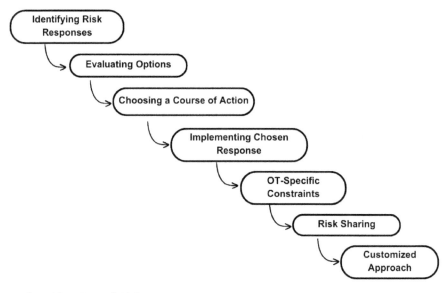

1. Identification of Risk Responses

The first step includes:

- **Recognition of OT-Specific Risks:** Understanding the inherent risks involved in the OT environment and developing practical solutions to these difficulties.

2. Evaluating Options

After finding potential replies, the following stage is to assess these possibilities:

- **Reviewing Identified Responses:** Involves assessing the feasibility and efficiency of each suggested solution.

- **Considering Organizational Risk Tolerance:** Integrate possible responses with the organization's risk tolerance, as specified by standards like IEC 62443.

3. Determine a course of action

Organizations must then choose the most suitable answer from among the alternatives offered.

- **Choosing between Acceptance, Avoidance, Mitigation, Sharing, or Transferring:** Determining the optimal plan for each identified risk in light of its possible impact and the organization's risk management rules.

4. Implementing the Chosen Response

Once a plan of action has been determined, it is time to:

- **Response into Action:** Executing the chosen approach to minimize the identified risk, which is managed by designated persons to guarantee timely and successful execution.

5. Considering OT-Specific Constraints:

Several elements can impact how risk responses are implemented in an OT environment:

- **System Requirements and Operational Impact:** Practical factors, such as the necessity to restart systems or the possibility of disrupting present activities, must be considered.

6. Sharing Risk.

In some cases, sharing risks can be an appropriate choice.

- **Collaboration Among Entities:** For instance, electricity-producing units may agree to share trained workers during an emergency to reduce operational effects.

7. Customized Approach:

Finally, it is critical to personalize the response to the unique demands and problems of the OT context:

- **Tailoring Responses:** Understanding that each system and scenario may necessitate a unique strategy, taking into account the various qualities and needs of OT systems.

Successfully responding to OT security concerns necessitates a strict and adaptable strategy, from finding and evaluating practical options to implementing and customizing solutions based on individual operational demands and restrictions. Following these systematic procedures can help organizations improve their capacity to manage security risks in OT settings, assuring the continuity, safety, and security of critical infrastructure operations. This technique not only helps to mitigate immediate risks but also improves the long-term resilience and dependability of OT systems.

5.6 MONITORING RISK

Monitoring risk in Operational Technology (OT) settings is essential for ensuring the security and reliability of key systems. An organized strategy offers ongoing protection against emerging threats and weaknesses. This section describes the key actions and considerations involved in monitoring OT security concerns.

Monitoring Risk

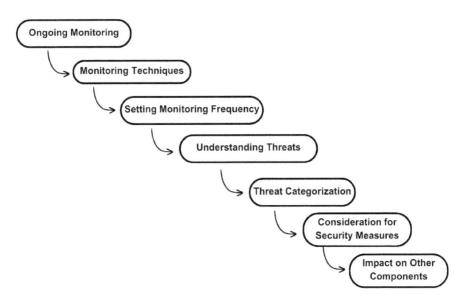

1. Ongoing Monitoring

Continuous attentiveness is required for:

- **Evaluating the Effectiveness of Management Strategies:** Regularly assessing the effectiveness of security measures that have been deployed.
- **Adapting to Changes:** Responding to changes in asset inventory or environmental conditions that may affect risk levels.

2. Monitoring Techniques

Choosing the appropriate monitoring techniques involves:

- **Balancing Passive and Active Monitoring:** While passive monitoring is non-intrusive, active or manual monitoring may be required to ensure complete data correctness.
- **Engineering Considerations:** Detailed preparation is essential to guarantee that monitoring operations do not disrupt operating processes.

3. Monitoring Frequency.

Determining how frequently to monitor relies on:

- **Risk Profile Customization:** Creating a monitoring plan based on the criticality and susceptibility of various OT systems.
- **Operational Constraints:** To prevent disturbance, align monitoring operations with operating schedules and system criticality.

4. Understanding Threats

Awareness of possible risks necessitates:

- **Industry-Specific Focus:** Focusing on threats particular to a given sector or operating environment.
- **External Expertise:** Consider using third-party services for specialized threat analysis and insight.

5. Threat Categorization

To effectively manage risks, it is important to:

- **Analyze the Likelihood and Impact:** Prioritizing risks based on their likelihood and possible impact on the organization.
- **Relevance to the Organization:** Focusing on dangers with immediate consequences for the OT environment while ignoring unimportant external happenings.

6. Security Measure Considerations

When installing security technology, consider the following:

- **Compatibility with OT Environments: Ensure** that new IT-based security solutions, such as antivirus software or Security Information and Event Management SIEM systems, are compatible with and authorized for usage in OT environments.
- **Operational Impact Assessment:** Assessing the possible impact of security measures on system availability and operational efficiency.

7. Impact of Monitoring on Risk Management

Effective monitoring impacts the whole risk management process by:

- **Improving Risk Assessment Accuracy:** Providing current information to enhance risk evaluations and management techniques.

- **Influencing Security Measures:** Guiding the selection and deployment of protective technologies and processes.

Monitoring OT security risk is a dynamic and necessary technique that supports successful risk management in critical technology environments. Organizations may maintain the adaptability and integrity of their operating technology by constantly assessing risk, changing monitoring techniques, identifying and categorizing risks, and carefully choosing security solutions. This proactive strategy allows for fast reactions to new threats and changes to security tactics, protecting critical systems from possible interruptions and intrusions.

5.7 APPLYING RISK MANAGEMENT FRAMEWORK

The National Institute of Standards and Technology (NIST) Risk Management Framework (RMF) outlines a thorough approach for incorporating risk management principles into system and organizational security operations. This framework is detailed in National Institute of Standards and Technology (NIST) Special Publication NIST SP 800-82 and guides organizations through the risk management process for operational technology (OT) and information technology (IT) systems. In this section, we look at the NIST RMF's basic processes to provide a clear knowledge of its application.

The Six Steps to NIST RMF

Risk Management Framework Steps

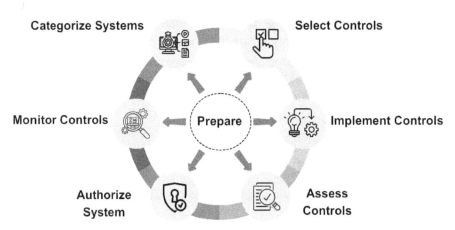

The RMF is based on six essential phases aimed at carefully addressing and managing risks:

- **Categorize System:** The first stage is to determine the system's impact level, which is often based on the type of information it processes and the potential consequences of a security breach. This category helps to prioritize security efforts and acquire relevant safeguards.

- **Select Controls:** After categorizing the system, applicable security measures are chosen to minimize the identified threats. These controls are designed to address the system's particular risk profile and operating requirements.

- **Implement Controls:** Once selected, the chosen security controls are implemented in the system. This stage comprises both the technical installation of controls and the documenting of control implementation methods.

- **Assess Controls:** Following implementation, the effectiveness of these controls is assessed using testing, auditing, and, in certain situations, penetration testing. This evaluation confirms that controls are operating properly to limit risks.

- **Authorize Systems:** A senior authority evaluates the assessment results and other necessary paperwork to determine whether the system's risks are acceptable. On evaluation, the system is authorized to operate, indicating that it meets specified security criteria.

- **Monitor Controls:** The final phase is regular monitoring of security measures to ensure they remain effective over time. This continual evaluation procedure enables revisions in response to changing threats and operating conditions.

Application of the RMF

Applying the RMF to operational technology OT and information technology (IT) systems comprises:

- **Prioritization Based on Impact:** System categorization allows resources to be directed toward preserving assets that are most critical first.

- **Tailored Security Measures:** Selecting and implementing controls that are specially designed to meet the system's operational and risk profile.

- **Continuous Improvement:** Regularly analyzing and monitoring controls promotes a dynamic security posture that adapts to the threat landscape and technology improvements.

The NIST Risk Management Framework provides a systematic strategy for finding, analyzing, responding to, and monitoring hazards in OT and IT systems. Organizations may develop a strong risk management process by following six steps: categorizing systems, selecting controls, implementing controls, assessing controls, authorizing systems, and monitoring controls. This framework not only improves system security and perseverance, but also guarantees that risk management activities are consistent, thorough, and in line with organizational goals. The RMF enables organizations to strike a balance between operational efficiency and security, assuring the continuing protection of vital technological infrastructures.

Risk Management Framework Steps

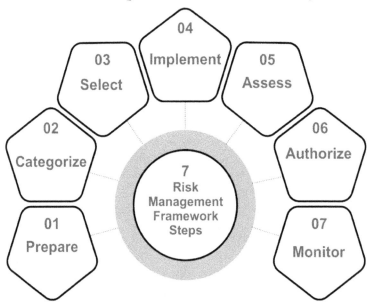

6.1 INTRODUCTION: RISK MANAGEMENT FRAMEWORK

This chapter details the Risk Management Framework Steps offering a guide on overseeing risks in an organizations activities. It explains each stage of the risk management procedure; Prepare, Categorize, Select, Implement, Assess, Authorize and Monitor. These stages create an interconnected approach that's vital for recognizing, evaluating and addressing risks. The section underscores the significance of this organized framework in guaranteeing the security, compliance and resilience of business activities. Grasping these stages is essential for students as it equips them to deploy risk management approaches in real-world situations enhancing the security stance of their future workplaces.

6.2 PREPARE

The process of preparation is the starting point of the NIST Risk Management Framework (RMF), providing a comprehensive approach to resolving security and privacy issues inside an organization. This initial phase establishes the framework for effectively dealing with the complexity of risk management, with a focus on the National Institute of Standards and Technology NIST SP 800-82 recommendations for OT systems. The preparation phase includes several essential tasks and considerations intended to ensure that an organization is well-equipped to tackle security and privacy concerns.

Key Actions for Comprehensive Readiness

The basis for risk management consists of many important steps:

- **Identifying Critical Assets:** Determine which systems, data, and resources are critical to the organization's operations.

- **Managing Risk Appetite:** Defining the degree of risk that the organization is ready to bear in achieving its goals.

- **Securing Necessary Funding:** Allocating funds to assist risk management activities.

Organizational-Level Engagement

Effective risk management involves active engagement from senior management in:

- **Develop and Implement Risk Management Planning:** Creating a risk management strategy that is integrated with organizational procedures and culture.

- **Integration with Organizational Culture and Governance:** Ensure that risk management concepts are ingrained in the organizational structure.

Mission and Business Operations Considerations

Understanding how security and privacy issues affect the organization's primary goal comprises:

- **Identifying Critical Business and Mission Functions:** Documenting critical operations and the data flows that enable them.

- **Outlining the Protection Mechanisms:** Defining what constitutes successful security measures in terms of supporting the organization's mission.

System-specific Focus

To design protection tactics, it is necessary to investigate the details of an organization's systems.

- **Documenting Existing Systems:** Creating an inventory of all systems and their currently operational security mechanisms.

- **Assessing the Effectiveness of Protection Measures:** Evaluating how effectively present security measures are working.

- **Defining System Boundaries:** Clarifying what is included in each system's domain.

The Risk Management Framework (RMF) provides a systematic method for addressing security and privacy issues.

- **Providing a Framework for Action:** The RMF provides organizations with the mechanisms needed to analyze, respond to, and monitor risks.

- **Ensure Accurate and Proactive Risk Management:** Organizations that have carefully planned may confidently use the RMF to manage risks with accuracy and anticipation.

The preparation phase is an essential component of the NIST RMF, laying the groundwork for a successful risk management program. Organizations can create a secure and proactive environment by identifying critical assets, engaging senior management, considering the impact on mission and business operations, focusing on system-specific requirements, and effectively employing the RMF. This foundational phase ensures that organizations are prepared to face the difficulties of protecting OT systems, using NIST SP 800-82 advice to improve resilience against attacks while maintaining their core purpose and operations.

6.3 P-1: RISK MANAGEMENT ROLES

Operational Technology (OT) systems are crucial for the operation of many important infrastructures, ranging from industrial plants to energy-generating facilities. Effective risk management in these systems is critical to ensuring their security, dependability, and availability. Identifying and assigning particular roles and duties is a critical component of the risk management process, as defined in NIST SP 800-82. This guarantees that an organization's cybersecurity approach is organized, with clear responsibilities, especially when dealing with external parties.

Key Roles in Operational Technology OT Risk Management

Establishing clear roles does not mean assigning labels, but rather developing a thorough framework in which the tasks of each function are fully defined:

- **Process Plant Manager:** Manages the whole facility's operations, ensuring that everything works smoothly and efficiently.

- **Process Control Engineer:** Ensures the smooth running of machinery and systems by utilizing computer technology to maintain control processes.

- **Operator:** Often referred to as the "mechanics guy," this position requires hands-on operations and immediate monitoring of the machinery and technology systems.

- **Functional Safety Engineer:** Also known as the "firewall guy," is in charge of creating and maintaining cybersecurity safeguards to defend systems from attacks.

- **Maintenance Personnel: They** are responsible for the upkeep and maintenance of OT systems, ensuring they are operational and secure.

- **Process Safety Manager:** Serves as the "protector," concentrating on the whole safety element of the operating environment, including cybersecurity risks.

Organizational Structure and Cybersecurity Accountability

This framework is about establishing an organized decision-making system that does more than just assign responsibilities.

- **Assigns Duties:** Clearly defines duties for people or teams within the organization, ensuring that everyone understands their unique cybersecurity tasks.

- **Harmonizes Strategy:** The goal is to combine various functions into a united strategy for fighting cyber threats, therefore improving the organization's overall security posture.

- **Establishes a Security Wall:** Provides a strong defense against vulnerabilities and threats that jeopardize the continuity and safety of key infrastructures, ensuring the resilience of operating technologies.

Identifying roles and responsibilities in OT risk management is a vital step toward protecting critical infrastructures from cyber-attacks. As part of the NIST SP 800-82 recommendations, this organized approach to job assignment guarantees that every component of the OT system's security is carefully designed and controlled. Organizations may construct a unified and successful plan for minimizing cyber risks by creating clear responsibilities and designating particular responsibilities, improving the security and dependability of critical operational systems.

6.4 P-2: RISK MANAGEMENT STRATEGY

Developing a risk management strategy is an important first step in assuring the safety, security, and continuity of operations inside businesses, particularly those that rely significantly on operational technology (OT) systems. This strategy, as outlined in NIST SP 800-82, includes a planned approach to recognizing, analyzing, and responding to risks or threats that may affect a company's operations. The following sections describe the critical components of building a successful risk management plan for OT situations.

Establishing Risk Tolerance

A risk management strategy begins with:

- **Identifying the Company's Risk Tolerance:** Understanding what risks the organization is willing to take to achieve its business objectives is critical. This involves deciding the degree of risk that the firm is ready to accept to achieve its objectives.

Developing the Strategy

An in-depth understanding of risk tolerance allows the organization to:

- **Outline Risk Management Approaches:** Determine which risks to accept, avoid, transfer, or mitigate using particular principles and actions. This stage is critical for prioritizing risk management activities depending on the company's ability to manage risk.

Developing a Risk Management Plan

After deciding on a risk-management strategy, the following stage is:

- **Developing a Risk Management Plan:** This document describes how the identified risks will be managed under the company's general business strategy and risk tolerance inventory. It provides thorough guidance for ensuring a secure and risk-aware operational environment.

Implementing Top-Down Objectives

The strategy and plan are guided by:

- **Top-Down, Goal-Oriented Objectives:** Ensuring that the risk management strategy and plan are aligned with the company's overall goals and are executed throughout the organization in a top-down manner.

Creating a Risk Management Strategy in the context of OT comprises a thorough assessment of the company's risk tolerance, followed by strategic planning for how to manage these risks following the company's business objectives. The resultant Risk Management Plan serves as an important guideline for the organization, outlining how risks should be handled across all business models and processes.

6.5 P-3: RISK ASSESSMENT – ORGANIZATION

Risk assessment in the context of Operational Technology (OT) systems is not something that can be done once and then ignored. According to NIST SP 800-82 recommendations, risk assessment is critical for every organization's long-term security and operational integrity. This section emphasizes the necessity of ongoing risk assessment and the requirement for organizations to adapt to changing threats and vulnerabilities over time.

Continuous Reassessment

Risk assessment at the organizational level includes:

- **Regular Reevaluation:** Businesses must review their risk assessments regularly. This guarantees that new or emerging risk factors do not catch the organization unprepared.

- **Monitoring Residual Risk: It** is crucial to assess if the amount of residual risk is within acceptable limits after applying security measures to ensure operational security.

- **Adapting Mitigation Strategies:** To meet the changing threat landscape, the efficiency of existing risk-mitigation devices and processes must be continually examined and improved.

Keeping Up with Business and Technological Evolution

The changing nature of the corporate environment, as well as technical improvements, require:

- **Assessment, Examination, and Improvement:** This cyclical process enables firms to be alert to emerging challenges and adjust their risk management methods accordingly.

- **Addressing New Vulnerabilities:** As the business environment changes, new vulnerabilities may develop or the nature of current risks may shift, necessitating an adjustment to organizations' risk assessment and mitigation techniques.

Risk assessment at the organizational level, as described in NIST SP 800-82, is a continuous process that needs constant attention and modification. Organizations must commit to continuously reassessing their risk profiles and altering their security measures in response to new knowledge and changing situations. By doing so, organizations can guarantee that their OT systems are safe against both present and future threats, preserving their integrity and continuity.

6.6 P-4: TAILORED CONTROL BASELINE AND CYBERSECURITY FRAMEWORK

To provide security and resilience against cyber -in OT systems, a general strategy is required. Following NIST SP 800-82 principles, project P-4 highlights the necessity of building control baselines and cybersecurity framework profiles that are suitable to each enterprise. This stage is critical for developing security measures that are specifically tailored to each organization's operational demands, technical settings, and cybersecurity threats. We will understand how to customize these important components to improve the efficiency of risk management strategies.

Tailoring Control Baselines

Control baselines are the core principles for information and system security. Customizing these baselines includes:

- **Assessing Organizational Needs:** Understanding the organization's particular operational requirements as well as its technology landscape.
- **Identifying Unique Challenges:** Recognize the organization's particular cybersecurity challenges.

Integrating Cybersecurity Framework Profiles

Combining customized control baselines with standard cybersecurity framework profiles enables enterprises to:

- **Ensure Industry Standard Compliance:** Customizing controls ensures that security policies not only meet industry standards but are also tailored to the organization's unique risk landscape.
- **Address Specific Threats:** Customizing allows businesses to employ cybersecurity measures that directly combat the identified threats, rather than using broad, ineffective solutions.

The Tailored Approach to Cybersecurity

The technique of tailoring cybersecurity measures has various advantages:

- **Focused Risk Management:** Tailored controls and framework profiles result in more effective risk management procedures that suit the organization's specific goals and difficulties.
- **Enhanced Security Assurance:** Organizations may be certain that their cybersecurity measures are both industry-compliant and tailored to guard against their specific threats.
- **Adaptability to the Environment:** Customized cybersecurity measures guarantee that protection tactics are tailored to the exact requirements of the operating environment, increasing resilience and security.

Organizations that rely on OT systems must implement a customized strategy to control baselines and cybersecurity framework profiles, as specified in NIST SP 800-82. Companies may achieve more effective and targeted risk management by modifying these features to meet the unique demands and difficulties of their operational and technical environments. This tailored strategy not only assures compliance with industry standards but also improves the organization's capacity to defend against unique cyber threats, ensuring the continuity and integrity of vital operating technology.

6.7 P-5: COMMON CONTROL IDENTIFICATION

In terms of Operational Technology (OT) system security, as stated in NIST SP 800-82, Project P-5 highlights the need to identify and implement standard cybersecurity procedures throughout an organization. This project emphasizes the need to create fundamental security concepts that are generally applicable inside the company, while also acknowledging the need for adapted methods related to the particular security requirements of various technology environments. Below, we will understand the strategic process of identifying and implementing common controls.

Identifying Universal Cybersecurity Measures

The identification of common controls includes:

- **Universal Security Methods:** Identifying cybersecurity concepts and methods that can be implemented uniformly across all devices, systems, and data in the company.

- **Simplification of Cybersecurity Efforts**: The goal of implementing common controls is to streamline the cybersecurity process, improving the overall coherence and effectiveness of the organization's security posture.

Tailoring Implementation to Different Security Needs

While common controls offer a basis, it is critical that:

- **Exercise Discretion:** Recognize that not all security measures are appropriate for all types of technology utilized by the firm.

- **Customize Controls:** Modify the application of these generic controls to the individual security requirements of different infrastructures inside the company.

Need for a Balanced Approach

The study emphasizes the significance of a balanced cybersecurity approach.

- **Avoiding One-Size-Fits-All Solutions:** A broad approach to cybersecurity might result in certain regions being under-protected, while others face unreasonable constraints.

- **Achieving Optimal Security:** By identifying common controls and tailoring their implementation to unique needs, companies may guarantee that all areas are sufficiently protected without sacrificing functionality or efficiency.

Project P-5, as directed by NIST SP 800-82, emphasizes the importance of common control identification in improving the cybersecurity framework of businesses that use OT systems. Organizations may create a more integrated and successful cybersecurity strategy by implementing universal cybersecurity measures and adapting their execution to meet the varying security demands of various technologies. This balanced approach not only streamlines the security management process but also guarantees that protection mechanisms are adequately scaled, preventing both under- and over-protection throughout the organization's technological environment.

6.8 P-6: Impact-Level Prioritization

Project P-6 demonstrates the relevance of impact-level priority in NIST SP 800-82 and operational technology (OT) system security. This approach involves executing a strategic review and alignment of all Information Technology (IT) and Operational Technology systems based on their importance to an organization's operational procedures and possible influence on safety and service delivery. The goal is to guarantee those systems critical to sustaining vital operating capabilities or protecting workers and the public receive more attention and resources. The approach and aims of impact-level prioritizing are described below.

Assessing System Criticality

The procedure includes:

- **Thorough Analysis:** Conducting an in-depth review to determine the criticality of systems within the organization's operating framework.

- **Understanding the Impact on Operations:** Determine how the interruption of these systems may influence organizational functions, worker safety, and public well-being.

System Prioritization by Impact

- **High-Impact Systems:** Identifying systems, particularly those connected to OT, whose functioning is important to sustaining critical organizational competencies and assuring safety.

- **Resource Allocation:** Concentrating protective resources and cybersecurity measures on these high-impact systems.

Influencing Protective Measures

Prioritization directly influences security strategies:

- **Enhanced Risk Management:** Implementing comprehensive risk management methods specifically designed to protect high-impact systems.

- **Investment in Cybersecurity:** Allocate a higher portion of cybersecurity funds to secure critical infrastructure, ensuring adequate defensive mechanisms are in place.

NIST SP 800-82 recommends impact-level prioritizing as a strategic approach to operational technology systems security. Organizations may successfully prioritize their protective efforts by carefully examining the criticality of IT and OT systems, as well as their potential influence on organizational operations and safety. This priority ensures that resources are distributed efficiently, focusing on systems whose compromise would have the most negative impact. This method not only improves the security and resilience of key infrastructure components, but also helps to ensure that important services run continuously, safely, and reliably.

6.9 P-7: CONTINUOUS MONITORING STRATEGY – ORGANIZATION

- Project P-7, "Continuous Monitoring Strategy – Organization," aligns with NIST SP 800-82 and focuses on developing a comprehensive strategy to continually safeguard and preserve the integrity of an organization's information technology (IT) and operational technology (OT) systems. This method is critical for ensuring that cybersecurity measures stay effective over time while responding to new threats and vulnerabilities that emerge.

Development of an Evaluation Framework

The key components of a continuous monitoring approach include:

- **Developing an Evaluation Framework:** This framework is intended to continuously monitor and review the efficiency of existing cybersecurity measures, ensuring that they are durable and up to date.

Key Realizations

The approach seeks to achieve two primary objectives:

- **Identifying Vulnerabilities:** Finding any security vulnerabilities or cracks in protection measures that might be exploited by cyber-attacks.

- **Assessing Defense Robustness:** Evaluating cybersecurity measures' strength and resilience to make sure they remain unaffected by changes in the threat landscape.

Monitoring Processes for IT Infrastructure

In IT settings, monitoring includes:

- **Network Traffic Analysis:** Identifying illegal communications that may signal a security compromise.

- **Security Log Review:** To identify unexpected actions that may indicate an intrusion or attempt at one.

- **Vulnerability Assessments:** Conducting accurate assessments to identify vulnerabilities, followed by applying the most recent updates to reduce these risks.

OT System Monitoring

For OT systems, notably in the industrial and manufacturing sectors, the emphasis extends to:

- **Physical Security Measures Monitoring:** Ensuring that physical barriers and controls successfully prevent unauthorized entry or manipulation.

- **System Integrity and Resilience Assessment:** Assessing the OT systems' capacity to survive environmental disturbance while maintaining operational integrity.

Project P-7 highlights the significance of a dynamic continuous monitoring approach inside businesses, particularly those that rely on OT systems, as suggested by NIST SP 800-82. Organizations may proactively discover vulnerabilities, assess the efficacy of cybersecurity solutions, and maintain critical infrastructure resilience in an ever-changing threat landscape by creating a systematic review framework and leveraging multiple monitoring techniques. This strategy not only improves the security of IT and OT systems but also adds to businesses' overall preparation and resilience in the face of increasing cyber threats, assuring the continuity and safety of critical operational processes.

6.10 P-8: MISSION OR BUSINESS FOCUS

Project P-8, as detailed in NIST SP 800-82, emphasizes the important relevance of aligning information technology (IT) and operational technology (OT) systems with an organization's purpose and overall business objectives. This alignment demands a thorough evaluation of information flows and interactions between IT and OT systems, as well as precise documentation and adherence to the particular standards that govern their collaboration. Understanding the critical stages for attaining this alignment and ensuring that IT and OT infrastructures not only support but also improve the organization's purpose and business operations.

Examination and Documentation

The procedure includes:

- **Thorough Examination**: Examining how information is transferred between IT and OT systems to uncover inefficiencies or misalignment with company objectives.
- **Comprehensive Documentation:** Keeping complete records of all components of the IT and OT systems, including data flows and the legal environment that influences system collaboration.

Reasons for Comprehensive Documentation

The need for extensive documentation arises from two main objectives:

- **Protecting Organizational Integrity:** Ensuring that all aspects of the IT and OT infrastructure are built and operational in a way that supports the organization's core objective.
- **Protecting Against Weaknesses:** Identifying possible system vulnerabilities that might harm the organization's goals and implementing proactive mitigation measures.

BENEFITS OF ALIGNING IT AND OPERATIONS WITH BUSINESS GOALS

The alignment of IT and OT systems with business objectives allows firms to:

- **Utilize Resources Efficiently:** By understanding corporate goals and procedures, businesses may better spend their limited resources, focusing on areas that have the greatest direct influence on their purpose.

- **Improve Operational Resilience**: A comprehensive understanding of business goals enables better preparedness for managing vulnerabilities, hence boosting the organization's capacity to respond to crises and difficulties.

- **Maintain a Responsive Stance:** Ensuring that IT and OT systems help to achieve business objectives keeps the firm nimble and focused on its purpose.

Project P-8 highlights the need to align IT strategically and OT systems with an organization's purpose and business objectives, as recommended by NIST SP 800-82. Organizations may guarantee that their technical infrastructures are not only compliant but also ideally structured to support essential activities and objectives by conducting a thorough audit, providing detailed documentation, and adhering to applicable legislation. This alignment is critical for maintaining organizational integrity, defending systems from possible threats, and maximizing resource utilization, ensuring that IT and OT systems actively contribute to business success.

6.11 P-9: SYSTEM STAKEHOLDERS

Project P-9, following the standards of NIST SP 800-82, highlights the essential procedure of systematically identifying and interacting with stakeholders in the Operational Technology (OT) ecosystem. Recognizing and reaching out to stakeholders is critical for incorporating multiple perspectives into the system's supervision, decision-making processes, and security policy development. We will discuss the importance of stakeholder identification and the roles that these stakeholders play in improving the integration and effectiveness of an organization's OT system.

Identification of stakeholders

The procedure includes:

- **Broad Stakeholder Scope:** Identifying persons and groups who engage with the OT system, either directly in terms of operation and safety (such as Process/Plant Managers and Process Safety Managers) or indirectly through the use of system outputs.

- **Recognizing Stakeholders:** It is a critical first step in ensuring their perspectives is taken into account, resulting in a more accessible and complete approach to system management.

Objectives of Stakeholder Engagement

Effective stakeholder involvement seeks to:

- **Facilitate Open Communication:** Establish avenues for regular and open communication among stakeholders, promoting mutual understanding and collaboration.

- **Identify Responsibilities:** Identifying each stakeholder's duties and responsibilities concerning the OT system will improve accountability and efficiency.

- **Encourage Shared Responsibility:** Fostering a culture of shared responsibility among stakeholders, in which each party contributes their experience and knowledge to achieve common security and operational goals.

- **Incorporate Diverse Experiences:** Use stakeholders' diverse experiences and ideas to address and reduce security concerns at the local, state, and national levels.

Project P-9 highlights the strategic relevance of identifying and engaging stakeholders in the OT environment, as suggested by NIST SP 800-82. Organizations may guarantee that a diverse range of viewpoints and skills are included in OT system management and security policies by conducting systematic identification and active outreach. This collaborative approach not only improves the decision-making process but also connects the functioning of OT systems with the organization's overall goals. As a result, the OT system's performance improves meeting or exceeding all stakeholders' expectations and interests.

6.12 P-10: ASSET IDENTIFICATION

Project P-10 underlines the importance of Asset Identification in relation to NIST SP 800-82 and the larger framework of risk management within Operational Technology (OT) systems. This procedure is a careful process of identifying, recording, and analyzing vital assets required for the continuing functioning and security of a company's OT environment. These assets include essential components such as Programmable Logic Controllers (PLCs) in manufacturing and industrial environments, as well as sensors, software, and network routers that enable the sophisticated communication networks that exist throughout operational technologies. Understanding the stages and factors involved in asset identification, as well as its role in risk management strategy.

Steps for Asset Identification

Asset identification involves the following steps:

- **Identifying Critical Assets:** Identifying the components required for the operation of the OT system, such as control systems, sensors, firmware, and communications infrastructure.
- **Documentation:** Keeping complete records of recognized assets, including their functions, locations, and responsibilities in the OT environment.

Assessing Asset Value

Once the assets are discovered, they are evaluated based on:

- **Contribution to Operations:** Evaluating each asset's influence on the entire process and operational continuity.
- **Failure Impact:** Taking into account the potential effects of asset failure on the organization's operations and safety.
- **Security Breach Implications:** Determine the degree of the impact that a security breach would have on each asset.

Prioritizing Assets

The evaluation leads to the following:

- **Resource Allocation:** Enabling the business to properly allocate resources while prioritizing the protection of its most important assets.
- **Efficient Risk Management:** Managing the prioritizing of cybersecurity measures to protect assets critical to the organization's performance and operational integrity.

Project P-10, which is directed by NIST SP 800-82, highlights the importance of Asset Identification in the security and risk management of operational technology systems. Organizations may establish a more focused and efficient risk management approach by carefully identifying, recording, and analyzing the value of essential assets. This method not only helps to prioritize cybersecurity efforts and resource allocation, but it also makes sure that protective measures are focused on preserving the components that are most critical to operational continuity and success. As a result, Asset Identification is an essential step in developing a strong risk management strategy that ensures the resilience and security of important OT infrastructures.

6.13 P-11: AUTHORIZATION BOUNDARY

Project P-11, also known as the Authorization Boundary, has significance towards the cybersecurity architecture for operational technology (OT) systems, as specified in NIST SP 800-82. This process requires setting clear limits within which system-specific permissions, such as user access rights, roles, and privileges, are recognized and implemented. Establishing an authorization boundary is critical for developing safe operating environments because it specifies exactly where and how interactions with the system take place depending on user credentials. Understanding the important features of establishing an authorization boundary and its importance in improving system security.

Establishing System-Specific Permissions

The method involves:

- Defining Secure Frameworks: Specifying the specific settings under which permissions are enabled, as well as directing who has access to and interacts with certain elements of the system.
- **Implementing Rights and Privileges:** Clearly defining users' rights and roles inside the authorization boundary to enable adequate access management.

Derived from cybersecurity strategy

The authorization boundary is formulated according to:

- **Strategic Planning:** Coordinating with the organization's cybersecurity plan to prevent unauthorized access and mitigate the effects of security incidents.
- **Regulatory Compliance:** Ensuring that actions within the border are under security rules and regulatory regulations, which is especially important in complex IT and operational contexts.

Goals of the Authorization Boundary

The createon of an authorized border attempts to:

- **Protect Critical Data and Processes:** Controlling access to key operational data and processes to ensure their confidentiality and integrity.
- **Minimize Unauthorized Access:** By explicitly establishing the permission boundary, companies may successfully prevent unauthorized users from accessing sensitive system components.
- **Compliance and Security:** Monitoring and managing activities within the border to ensure compliance with enterprise security policies and regulatory responsibilities.

According to NIST SP 800-82, the Authorization Boundary is a vital component of the risk management approach for operational technology systems. It assures critical infrastructure security. By clearly outlining the restrictions for system access and interactions based on user credentials, companies may build a more secure environment that protects against unauthorized access and fits with cybersecurity policies. This fundamental activity is critical for preserving the confidentiality, integrity, and availability of operational technology systems, as well as ensuring that they run inside secure and regulated frameworks that comply with corporate security policies and regulatory mandates.

6.14 P-12: INFORMATION TYPES

Project P-12, named "Information Types," is an important phase in an organization's data governance and cybersecurity architecture, directed by NIST SP 800-82. This activity includes the careful breakdown and categorization of all data handled by an organization's systems, such as data collecting, processing, storage, and transfer. Data categorization into particular categories depending on the type and sensitivity of the information is critical for developing targeted security measures and complying with data privacy legislation. Understanding the process of determining information categories and the importance of this classification in developing an effective data governance program.

Classifying Data

The classifying process includes:

- **Identifying Data Categories:** Depending on their qualities and sensitivity, data can be classified as public, confidential, sensitive, personal, or proprietary.

- **Establishing Security Regulations:** Tailoring security measures to the categorization of data, ensuring that protection levels are adequate for the sensitivity of the information.

Purpose of Data Classification

Data categorization performs numerous important functions:

- **Enhancing Data Protection Compliance:** Ensuring that security processes fulfill the standards outlined in applicable data protection regulations, consequently protecting corporate resources.

- **Informing Risk Assessment:** Using knowledge of information kinds to properly estimate the risk level and potential consequences of hypothetical data breaches.

- **Forming Data Governance Programs:** Creating strong data governance frameworks that incorporate elements such as data integrity, confidentiality, and availability based on the classified information kinds.

Importance of Understanding Information Types

Understanding the nature of the information that an organization manages is important for:

- **Effective Data Management:** Enables the development of specific plans for data management, storage, and protection.

- **Cybersecurity Strategy Development:** Guides the development of cybersecurity measures that are appropriate for the sensitivity and value of the data.

- **Mitigating Data Breach Impacts:** Helps the company respond more effectively to data breaches by knowing the possible hazards connected with various types of information.

The identification and categorization of information types, as specified in Project P-12 and suggested by NIST SP 800-82, are essential components of successful data governance and cybersecurity in any company. Organizations can better secure sensitive information by classifying data depending on its nature and sensitivity. This systematic approach to data categorization not only enables strong data governance programs, but also contributes to the organization's entire risk management strategy by protecting the integrity, confidentiality, and availability of its information assets.

6.15 P-13: INFORMATION LIFE CYCLE

Project P-13, called "Information Life Cycle," describes how data moves through an organization's Operational Technology (OT) system in accordance with NIST SP 800-82 criteria. This assignment illustrates the important steps that data goes through, from generation or capture to final archiving or disposal. Understanding the data's life cycle is critical for stakeholders to fully understand the nature of their interactions with data and the transformations it goes through across different hands. Below, we will look at the components of the information life cycle and how they contribute to data security, access, and integrity.

Phases of Information Life Cycle

The life cycle of information includes:

- **Data Creation or Capture:** The entry of data into the system, signaling the start of its journey.
- **Data Utilization:** The process of actively using and manipulating data for a variety of operational goals.
- **Data Storage:** The process of storing data while it is not in immediate use, which necessitates security and integrity precautions.
- **Data Sharing:** The process of transmitting data within or outside of an organization, which requires strong safeguards to prevent unwanted access.
- **Data Archiving or Disposal:** The last stage in which data is either securely stored for long-term storage or disposed of in a way that safeguards sensitive information.

Importance of Understanding the Data Life Cycle

Identifying each stage of the data life cycle enables businesses to:

- **Improve Data Security:** By identifying the most susceptible areas in data, companies may apply specific security measures to secure it throughout its life cycle.

- **Maintain Data Integrity:** Ensuring that data is correct and unmodified throughout its life cycle is critical for operational reliability.

- **Control Data Access:** Understanding the data flow allows for the implementation of strict access controls, ensuring that only authorized users interact with sensitive or regulated data.

- **Comply with Data Retention Laws:** Understanding the data life cycle helps you meet legal obligations for data retention, destruction, and archiving, ensuring regulatory compliance.

Project P-13, as indicated by NIST SP 800-82, highlights the essential idea of the Information Life Cycle in Operational Technology systems. Organizations may implement complex safeguards to protect data at every stage of their journey by revealing the path they follow from creation to disposal. This complete knowledge not only protects sensitive and regulated data but also assures compliance with data retention laws and other legal requirements. Finally, understanding the information life cycle is critical for ensuring data security, access, and integrity, which supports the organization's entire data governance and cybersecurity architecture.

6.16 P-14: RISK ASSESSMENT- SYSTEM

Project P-14, named "Risk Assessment - System," focuses on carefully evaluating and updating risk studies for operational technology (OT) systems in accordance with NIST SP 800-82 criteria. This work is crucial for evaluating the resilience and security of OT systems against possible cybersecurity threats without interfering with normal operations. These systems are critical for assuring the continuous operation of organizational activities and strengthening security measures throughout the company. Understanding the important components of doing a focused risk assessment for OT systems, as well as the strategic value of this work.

Conducting a Targeted Risk Assessment

The procedure includes:

- **Thorough Examination:** A thorough review of all areas of OT system operation to identify vulnerabilities and potential cybersecurity risks.

- **Non-Disruptive Implementation:** Ensure that the risk assessment procedure does not interfere with the normal operation of the OT systems.

Objectives of Risk Assessment for OT Systems

The major aims are:

- **Identifying Vulnerabilities:** Detecting weaknesses in OT systems that might be exploited by cyber-attacks.

- **Enhancing System Resilience:** Evaluating a system's capacity to resist and recover from cybersecurity events.

- **Maintaining Continuous Operation:** Ensuring that the OT infrastructure is functioning, hence protecting the organization's ability to function successfully.

Importance of Systematic Risk Assessment

Systematic risk assessment is necessary for:

- **Preventing Failures:** By detecting and resolving possible vulnerabilities, companies may avoid system failures that endanger cybersecurity.

- **Protecting Organizational Operations:** Securing the OT infrastructure from cyber-attacks is critical for ensuring the organization's operational capability.

- **Supporting Security Measures Development:** The findings from the risk assessment guide the creation and maintenance of strong security measures across the OT environment.

Project P-14 highlights the need to carry out an organized risk assessment for operational technology systems, as suggested by NIST SP 800-82. Organizations can discover possible vulnerabilities and apply actions to improve resilience against cybersecurity attacks by thoroughly examining the functioning of their OT systems. This focused analysis assures that the OT infrastructure stays safe and functioning, allowing the business to operate and secure itself continuously. By prioritizing non-disruptive installation, the risk assessment process protects against system disruptions, ensuring that organizational processes that rely on OT systems remain uninterrupted and secure.

6.17 P-15: REQUIREMENTS DEFINITION

Project P-15, named "Requirements Definition," is important for integrating strong security and privacy protections into operational technology (OT) systems in accordance with NIST SP 800-82 recommendations. This process involves systematically gathering and prioritizing security and privacy standards that the system must meet, guaranteeing full protection, and complying with business risk policies and plans. We will describe the process of determining these requirements and their importance in the safe and private functioning of OT systems.

Gathering Security and Privacy Benchmarks

The method involves:

- **Identifying Essential Standards:** Select the security standards and privacy norms that have been considered important to the organization's OT systems.

- **Benchmark Prioritization:** Organizing these standards and norms in order of relevance in accordance with the organization's risk policy and strategic objectives.

Creating Benchmarks

The essential phase includes:

- **Benchmark Development:** Create particular security and privacy benchmarks to assist the design, implementation, and operation of OT systems.

- **Alignment with Organizational Goals:** Ensuring that these standards are consistent with the organization's targeted security and privacy goals.

The Importance of Smart Prioritization

Prioritizing needs is necessary for:

- **Targeted Defensive Initiatives:** Prioritizing the most urgent and important threats, ensuring that defensive measures address the most important weaknesses.

- **Strategic Resource Allocation:** Allocating resources efficiently to where they are most required, hence improving the effectiveness of security and privacy controls.

Integrating Security and Privacy

The final objective of the requirements definition is to:

- **Ensure System Compliance:** Ensuring that all components of the OT systems meet specified security and privacy standards.

- **Integrating Security and Privacy:** Embedding these concepts into the system from the start, making them natural components of the system's architecture.

Project P-15 underscores the need to take a strategic approach to designing security and privacy requirements for operational technology systems, as recommended by NIST SP 800-82. Organizations may maintain the security and privacy of their OT systems by defining, prioritizing, and developing certain benchmarks. This procedure not only assures compliance with the organization's risk standards but also allows for logical prioritizing of defensive actions against the most serious risks. Finally, the Requirements Definition job establishes the groundwork for implementing strong security and privacy protections in OT systems, protecting vital infrastructure and sensitive data from growing cybersecurity threats.

6.18 P-16: ENTERPRISE ARCHITECTURE

Project P-16, "Enterprise Architecture," highlights the important integration of Operational Technology (OT) systems into the larger framework of an organization's architecture, following NIST SP 800-82 recommendations. This work serves as essential for defining the function and interconnectivity of the OT system inside the company, allowing for a more comprehensive approach to cybersecurity and operational efficiency. Understanding the process of integrating OT systems into corporate design, as well as the benefits of doing so.

Identifying the OT System's Role

The integration process includes:

- **Purpose and Relationship Identification:** Identifying the particular functions of the OT system and how they connect with other business components.

- **Component Classification:** Classifying the pieces that make up the OT system so that cybersecurity policies may be adjusted more efficiently.

Benefits of OT Integration in Enterprise Architecture

Integrating OT technologies with business architecture offers various benefits:

- **Enhanced Security Measures:** Allows for the construction of personalized security solutions for each OT component, taking into account its operational value and susceptibility to interruption.

- **Optimal Function Distribution:** Enables strategic distribution of organizational tasks and responsibilities, resulting in complete cybersecurity coverage.

- **Sustainable Cybersecurity Strategy:** Establishes the groundwork for a distinct and long-term strategy to defend the enterprise's OT infrastructure.

Importance of Understanding Enterprise Architecture

Understanding the corporate architecture is critical for:

- **Strengthening Security Systems:** An in-depth understanding of the enterprise layout improves the efficacy and resilience of security measures.

- **Strategic Planning and Reaction:** Enables strategic cybersecurity planning and quick reaction to attacks based on the criticality and functionality of various OT components.

Project P-16 highlights the need to carefully integrate operational technology systems into an organization's enterprise architecture, as suggested by NIST SP 800-82. Organizations may develop more effective, targeted cybersecurity strategies by understanding the function of OT components and mapping their interactions within the larger organizational architecture. This strategy not only improves the security posture of OT systems but also encourages an optimal allocation of roles and responsibilities throughout the company. Finally, understanding and executing enterprise architectural principles provides stronger protection against cyber threats by aligning operational technology systems with the organization's strategic goals and cybersecurity requirements.

6.19 P-17: REQUIREMENTS ALLOCATION

Project P-17, titled "Requirements Allocation," focuses on the strategic distribution of security and privacy needs across Operational Technology (OT) systems and their associated processes. Following NIST SP 800-82 recommendations, this activity is critical for incorporating these requirements in a way that strengthens system security and privacy without limiting the OT system's operation or undermining its fundamental safety measures. Understanding the strategy and relevance of successfully distributing these important requirements.

Strategic Allocation of Requirements

The allocation procedure involves:

- **Balancing Security and Performance:** Putting in place robust security measures to combat cybersecurity threats while ensuring that they do not have a negative impact on the OT system's operational efficiency or dependability.

- **Ensuring Safety Functionality:** Protecting the OT systems' inbuilt safety features, which are critical for avoiding accidents and preserving operational integrity.

Objectives of Requirement Allocation

This task seeks to:

- **Integrate Security Seamlessly:** Embedding security and privacy needs such that they become a natural extension of the OT system's activities, increasing protection levels while maintaining system performance.

- **Maintain Operational Effectiveness:** Retaining the OT systems' basic operational capabilities while ensuring that security measures do not impair system functioning or safety.

Importance of Thoughtful Requirements Integration

Effective requirement allocation is necessary for:

- **Protecting Against Cybersecurity Threats:** OT systems are protected against a wide range of cyber threats using well-integrated security solutions that are meant to be unnoticeable to system operations.

- **Maintaining System Safety and Privacy:** Making certain that the safety and privacy procedures inherent in OT systems are not undermined by the incorporation of additional security needs.

Project P-17 emphasizes the essential importance of properly assigning security and privacy requirements within operational technology systems, as recommended by NIST SP 800-82. Organizations may guarantee that their OT systems are both secure and effective by striking a careful balance between increasing security measures and preserving system performance and safety. This careful approach to needs allocation is critical for protecting OT infrastructures from developing cyber threats while maintaining the operational efficacy and safety aspects that are critical to the system's integrity. Finally, intelligent integration of security and privacy standards makes sure that OT systems continue to work properly, protected from any cyber threats without affecting vital capabilities.

6.20 P-18: SYSTEM REGISTRATION

Project P-18, entitled "System Registration," is a crucial operation within an organization's operating structure, according to NIST SP 800-82. It comprises the official identification and registration of operational technology (OT) systems inside the organizational structure. This stage plays an essential role in creating a clear structure for managing, administering, and assigning responsibilities and ownership of the OT systems. Understanding the fundamental components of system registration and its importance in organizational risk management and operational integrity.

Key Components of System Registration

The registration procedure comprises the following:

- **Identification and Documentation:** Carefully identifying and documenting each OT system in the organization, including its characteristics, operations, and security standards.

- **Ownership and Accountability:** Assigning ownership ensures that each system has a designated custodian who is accountable for its operation, security, and upkeep.

- **Regulatory Compliance and Tracking:** Enabling regulatory agencies to monitor the system's state, custodianship, and previous updates.

Objectives of System Registration

System registration attempts to:

- **Maintain an Inventory of Assets:** Keeping a current record of the organization's OT systems as part of the company's property portfolio.

- **Streamline Resource Allocation:** Efficient resource allocation is achieved by analyzing the distribution and requirements of each registered system.

- **Integrate into Risk Management**: Each system should be incorporated into the organization's broader risk management plan to reduce possible vulnerabilities and threats.

Benefits of System Registration

The process of registering OT systems inside a business provides several benefits.

- **Enhanced Security and Maintenance:** Implementing a systematic approach to the security and maintenance of OT systems based on documented ownership and responsibility.

- **Facilitated Post-Placement Assessments:** Allows for full assessments, modifications, and alignment of OT systems with the organization's changing demands and security standards.

- **Comprehensive Integration:** Ensuring that each OT system is examined in the context of the organization's systems and processes, resulting in operational harmony and efficiency.

Project P-18 highlights the necessity of the "System Registration" procedure, which is suggested by NIST SP 800-82, as a vital step in achieving operational technology system integration, accountability, and better security within an organization. By providing a clear framework for managing and administering OT systems, businesses can guarantee that these crucial resources are appropriately accounted for, securely maintained, and successfully incorporated into the broader risk management plan. The systematic registration of OT systems not only helps regulatory compliance and resource allocation but also creates the framework for continuing system assessments and alignments, therefore improving the organization's operational integrity and resistance to cybersecurity threats.

6.21 CATEGORIZE

The "Categorize" stage in the Risk Management Framework is essential for an extensive understanding and management of risks connected with Operational Technology (OT) systems, according to NIST SP 800-82. This core process focuses on examining the information system and the data it processes in order to estimate the possible impact of a security breach on the enterprise. It highlights the three key principles of information security: confidentiality, integrity, and availability, each of which plays an important role in ensuring the system's functioning and data integrity.

Fundamental Principles of Information Security

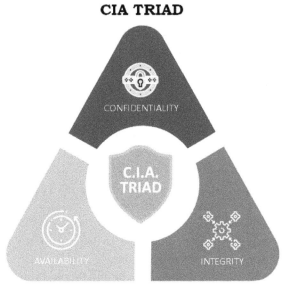

- **Confidentiality:** Ensures that sensitive information is not accessible to unauthorized persons or entities, protecting the organization's proprietary or confidential data from potential leaks or unlawful disclosure.

- **Integrity:** Ensures that data is accurate and reliable throughout its lifespan, from creation to disposal. Unauthorized modifications to data and removal, as well as operational mistrust, might all result from compromised integrity.

- **Availability:** Ensures that data and systems are available to authorized users as needed. Threats to availability, such as Distributed Denial of Service (DDoS) attacks can disrupt access to important data, severely affecting operations.

Goals of the Categorization Process

The categorizing procedure aims at:

- **Evaluate Incident Impact and Likelihood:** Determining the possible impact and likelihood of security events is crucial for developing an effective response strategy and choosing suitable security solutions.

- **Guide Security and Privacy Control Selection:** This stage is crucial for defining the appropriate security and privacy controls for the information system and aligning them with the organization's risk tolerance and compliance needs.

According to NIST SP 800-82, the "categorize" stage within the Risk Management Framework is crucial for Operational Technology systems. Organizations may strategically plan to install appropriate security and privacy measures by extensively examining the potential consequences of security breaches using the principles of confidentiality, integrity, and availability. This proactive strategy not only improves the safety of OT systems but also makes certain that the controls chosen are appropriate for the organization's overall risk tolerance and regulatory requirements. Finally, identifying risks efficiently creates the framework for a strong cybersecurity posture, allowing enterprises to protect their essential systems from emerging attacks.

6.22 TASK C-1: SYSTEM DESCRIPTION

Task C-1, often known as "System Description" or "documentation," is an essential part of any risk management or cybersecurity framework that follows the principles of NIST SP 800-82. This work seeks to provide a clear and integrated paper that covers a wide range of features of the operational technology (OT) system in question. The goal of creating this comprehensive documentation is multifaceted, including an explanation of the system's architecture, data flow patterns, interdependencies, and technology frameworks that support the system's operation.

Components of the System Description

- **Comprehensive Understanding:** The documentation should provide a comprehensive overview of the system, including its nature, purpose, and relevance to the organization's everyday activities.

- **Detailed Architecture Clarification:** It should describe the system's architecture, providing information about its structural composition and operational dynamics.

- **Data Flow and Interdependencies:** Understanding how information is handled and exchanged requires documentation of the system's data flow patterns as well as its interdependencies with other systems or processes.

- **Technological Frameworks:** The documentation must define the technological frameworks underlying the system, including any software, hardware, and network configurations.

Goals of System Description Documentation

The main purposes of creating a system description document are:

- **Facilitating Stakeholder Understanding:** Ensuring that stakeholders at all levels understand how the system works and the importance of the information it manages.

- **Informing Risk Management Processes:** Providing a basis for analyzing and managing information risks, allowing for more informed decisions on cybersecurity measures.

- **Enhancing Control Effectiveness:** Allowing the organization to evaluate the performance of installed controls, monitoring methods, and overall risk management strategy.

Task C-1 highlights the significance of properly documenting operational technology systems, as specified by NIST SP 800-82. By developing a complete system description, companies get a useful resource that improves knowledge of the system's functioning and position in the operational landscape. This paper is useful for stakeholders who are in charge of evaluating risks, developing cybersecurity strategies, and making educated control implementation decisions. Finally, a well-documented system description is essential for creating a strong cybersecurity posture, ensuring that OT systems are safeguarded from possible attacks while effectively serving the organization's objectives.

6.23 TASK C-2: SECURITY CATEGORIZATION

Task C-2, known as "Security Categorization," is a basic step in the field of operational technology (OT) risk management, as specified in NIST SP 800-82. This responsibility involves conducting a thorough examination of the organization's technical environment to better defend against any cybersecurity threats and vulnerabilities. The essence of security categorization is its capacity to analyze and categorize an organization's OT system security posture, showing the relationship between the organization's present security measures and its operational risk exposure.

Elements of Security Categorization

- **Comprehensive Security Review:** Conduct a complete evaluation to provide a detailed report that represents the organization's existing security landscape and how it aligns with overall business objectives.

- **Identification of Critical Segments:** Recognizing critical or susceptible sectors within the company that handle sensitive information and require special security care.

- **Risk Management Framework Alignment:** Ensure that the categorization process is aligned with the organization's risk management framework, highlighting the significance of protecting sensitive segments.

Goals of Security Categorization

The key objectives of doing a security classification include:

- **Determining Security Levels:** Setting suitable security levels based on the company's operational demands and risk tolerance to prevent data breaches and other cybersecurity issues.

- **Value and Risk Consideration:** Evaluating the underlying worth of various segments or operations within the firm and determining appropriate security measures to manage detected risks.

- **Enhancing Risk Management Strategies:** Using the insights acquired from security categorization to refine and improve the organization's risk management strategies, particularly in sensitive or important operating areas.

Task C-2 highlights the need for "Security Categorization" in the context of operational technology systems, as recommended by NIST SP 800-82. protection categorization allows enterprises to identify vulnerabilities, categorize the levels of protection required for distinct segments, and connect these measures with the broader risk management framework. This strategic approach not only allows for a better awareness of the existing security situation but also guides the creation of specific security solutions. Finally, security classification serves as essential for ensuring that OT systems are sufficiently safeguarded against possible attacks, thereby protecting the organization's operations and sensitive data.

6.24 TASK C-3: SECURITY CATEGORIZATION REVIEW AND APPROVAL

Task C-3, "Security Categorization Review and Approval," is an essential phase in the operational technology (OT) cybersecurity management system, as defined by NIST SP 800-82. This process comprises an in-depth review and approval of the previously defined security classification decisions for the organization's OT systems. It is a process that goes beyond simply selecting security solutions; it also includes verifying these decisions against the organization's overall security principles and objectives.

Key Features of Security Categorization Review and Approval

- **Intensive Examination:** Proposed security category choices are extensively evaluated to verify that they are flexible, efficient, and aligned with the organization's basic security goals.

- **Endorsement of Security Decisions:** Obtaining organizational support for cybersecurity strategies and actions determined as the best fit for securing the organization's systems.

- **Management Awareness and Endorsement:** Ensure that the organization's top management is completely aware of and supportive of the chosen security measures.

Objectives of Task C-3

The primary goals of performing a security category evaluation and approval procedure include:

- **Accountability and Transparency:** Holding the decision-making process for security measures responsible and transparent, in line with the organization's strategic goals.

- **Alignment with corporate Values:** Ensuring that the chosen security measures not only adequately solve security problems, but also reflect the corporate culture and values.

- **Facilitating Effective Implementation:** Enabling appropriate implementation and enforcement of security solutions with top management support, ensuring that these measures are realistic and durable.

Task C-3 is a key component of NIST SP 800-82's suggested strategic approach to cybersecurity in operational technology systems. By including top management in the evaluation and approval process, businesses ensure that the security category not only satisfies technical criteria but also matches the organization's strategic direction and values. This alignment becomes essential for successfully implementing and managing cybersecurity measures across OT systems. Finally, Task C-3 ensures that the security solutions implemented are not only technically robust but also have the required authorization and support to successfully integrate into the organization's operational structure.

6.25 SELECT

The "Select" step of the Risk Management Framework is a significant point at which businesses discuss the appropriate security procedures. This stage, which is consistent with NIST SP 800-82 advice, highlights the significance of selecting security measures that safeguard system information while simultaneously maintaining the system's operational efficacy. The selection process is a delicate balance that must be carefully considered to maintain the system's integrity and operation.

Essential Steps in the Selection Process

- **Exploration of Security Controls:** Organizations start by assessing the landscape of available security measures. Organizations can use frameworks like those provided by NIST to comprehend the many security measures at their disposal and select which solutions best suit their specific operating requirements.

- **Tailoring Controls to System Requirements:** It is critical that the recommended security controls are not implemented in a universally applicable way. Instead, they should be adapted to the system's demands, increasing machine efficiency while minimizing operating disturbances.

- **Operational Alignment:** The implementation of new security measures necessitates seamless interaction with current protocols and systems. This stage requires a collaborative effort between the organization's technical team and operational workers to ensure that the controls selected meet compliance requirements, operational goals, and security objectives.

Objectives of the Selection Phase

The main objective of the "Select" phase is to identify and install security policies that:

- **Maintain System Integrity and Functionality:** Ensure that the security measures do not interfere with the system's ability to execute its crucial duties.

- **Address Specific Security Needs:** Customize security measures to address the operational technology environment's specific risks and weaknesses.

- **Maintain Operational Efficiency:** Ensure that security measures improve, not restrict, operational efficiency.

NIST SP 800-82 recommends the "Select" step as a core component of a complete risk management approach for operational technology systems. Organizations may guard against possible attacks while maintaining the performance and usefulness of their operational technology by carefully choosing and configuring security measures to their systems' unique demands and operational environment. This delicate balancing act is essential for ensuring that OT systems remain secure and efficient while also supporting the organization's strategic objectives and operational demands.

6.26 TASK S-1: CONTROL SELECTION

Task S-1, "Control Selection," is a critical stage in the NIST SP 800-82-compliant cybersecurity management process for operational technology (OT) systems. Contrary to what the title suggests, this duty is more than just selecting security measures. Instead, it focuses on a strategic approach to determining the most effective security measures for an organization's OT systems. This decision-making process is heavily influenced by the results of the previous risk assessment phase and is essential to the organization's overall risk management strategy.

Key Components of Control Selection

- **Customization to OT Environment:** Security measures are adjusted to the particular characteristics of the OT environment, including its operational medium.

- **Alignment with Risk Management:** The selection process ensures that the chosen controls are consistent with the organization's risk management strategy, demonstrating a complete approach to minimizing any potential risks.

- **Standard Controls:** Organizations might use controls described in recognized standards or create custom measures to address their operational demands and threats.

Objectives of Task S-1

The purpose of this assignment is twofold:

- **Risk Mitigation:** Putting in place security measures that successfully decrease recognized risks to an acceptable level, therefore protecting the organization's assets from prospective attacks.

- **Operational Harmony:** Striking a delicate balance between achieving security standards and supporting the operational and safety demands of the OT environment. This assures that while security is improved, the functionality and integrity of OT operations are not affected.

Task S-1 demonstrates the difficulties of safeguarding operational technology systems. It underlines the importance of taking a nuanced approach when selecting security measures, taking into account the particular elements of the OT context. Organizations may protect their systems while maintaining performance by striking a compromise between strong security measures and operational requirements. This strategic alignment of security controls with the organization's risk management framework is vital for sustaining the resilience and integrity of OT systems in the face of increasing cybersecurity threats, according to NIST SP 800-82.

6.27 TASK S-2: CONTROL TAILORING

Task S-2, "Control Tailoring," looks into the essential procedure of tailoring traditional security controls to the individual demands and risk landscape of an organization's operational technology (OT) systems, in accordance with NIST SP 800-82 recommendations. This activity is crucial in ensuring that an organization's security architecture is not only strong and compatible with industry norms, but also sufficiently adaptable to handle specific operational issues and threat situations.

Core Elements of Control Tailoring

- **Customization of Security Controls:** Involves modifying security controls to fit an organization's operational architecture, technology, and risk profile.

- **Adaptation to Organizational Needs:** This approach allows the organization to investigate and apply alternative security solutions that may be more efficient or effective under the organization's particular conditions.

Objectives of Control Tailoring

The main goal of this activity is to create a security posture that:

- **Balances Risk and Performance:** Achieves an appropriate balance between protecting the OT environment from potential security risks and ensuring that system performance is not compromised.

- **Responds to unique threats:** Is agile and adaptable enough to address a wide range of security issues, according to the organization's unique operational and risk environment.

Task S-2 underlines the significance of customized solutions to security in the context of operational technology. Customizing security controls allows businesses to make sure that their defensive mechanisms are not just effective, but also personalized to support and improve operational efficiency. This balance is critical for ensuring the integrity and operation of OT systems while protecting them from cyber-attacks. Control tailoring, as stated in NIST SP 800-82, is crucial for developing a security architecture that is both resilient to threats and supportive of the organization's operational goals.

6.28 TASK S-3: CONTROL ALLOCATION

Task S-3, "Control Allocation," entails precisely distributing security controls throughout the various components of an organization's technical infrastructure using NIST SP 800-82 principles. This activity is critical in providing the system's complete protection by carefully assigning security procedures to segments based on their operational relevance, vulnerability levels, and the sensitivity of the data they manage.

Key Components of Control Allocation

- **Segment-Specific Security Protocols:** Customize security measures for each area of the technological infrastructure based on responsibilities, risk exposure, and data sensitivity.

- **Understanding System Architecture:** To successfully match security measures with areas of highest need, it is necessary to have a complete understanding of the system's structure, data flows, and possible vulnerabilities.

Objectives of Control Allocation

The main purpose of this work is to create a security posture that is:

- **Robust and Targeted:** Creates a powerful defensive mechanism by focusing increased security efforts on important or susceptible system components, therefore protecting sensitive processes and data.

- **Cost-effective Resource Utilization:** Ensures that security resources are used optimally by prioritizing regions that require the most demanding measures, resulting in an efficient deployment of protective efforts and minimal waste.

Task S-3 highlights the significance of a systematic approach to security in the operational technology landscape. By distributing controls based on an in-depth examination of the system's architecture and risk profile, companies can guarantee that their security posture is both formidable against threats and practical in its implementation. Control allocation, in accordance with NIST SP 800-82 guidelines, is critical for maintaining the integrity and functionality of OT systems, ensuring that the most critical or vulnerable areas receive the highest level of protection, and thus streamlining security investments to maximize impact.

6.29 TASK S-4: DOCUMENTATION OF PLANNED CONTROL IMPLEMENTATIONS

Task S-4, "Documentation of Planned Control Implementations," has importance to the operational technology (OT) risk management framework specified in NIST SP 800-82. This activity involves creating a clear and accessible record of the security measures that an organization intends to implement, including any adjustments customized to its unique operational environment.

Essential Documentation Components

- **Comprehensive Recording:** Details about the security procedures to be introduced are properly documented, including any organizational-specific changes.

The purpose of documentation is to:

- Serve as a starting point for the placement of controls.
- Provide explicit instructions for individuals performing the controls.
- Establish a foundation for future audits and compliance verifications.
- Ensure that the implementation process is transparent, both internally and to external regulators.

Objectives of Task S-4

This documentation effort emphasizes the following multidimensional objectives:

- **Facilitating Control Implementation:** Providing a clear design for the implementation of security measures.
- **Audit and Compliance Readiness:** Establishing an effective basis for future reviews and adherence checks by demonstrating the thinking process underlying control selections and adjustments.

- **Transparency and Accountability:** Maintaining open communication regarding security initiatives, and establishing trust among internal stakeholders and regulatory agencies.

- **Ensuring Continuity:** Documenting security policies and implementations helps to maintain the integrity of security measures during organizational transformations, such as changes in the system or workforce.

Task S-4's focus on documenting planned control measures is essential to a strong OT cybersecurity strategy. It not only confirms that the chosen security policies are properly understood and applied, but it also provides a framework for responsibility, transparency, and continuity. This material serves as the foundation for successful security management in the OT environment, aligned with NIST SP 800-82 requirements to ensure the operational integrity and compliance of the organization's IT systems.

6.30 TASK S-5: CONTINUOUS MONITORING STRATEGY - SYSTEM

Task S-5, "Continuous Monitoring Strategy - System," highlights an important part of operational technology (OT) risk management, in accordance with NIST SP 800-82 recommendations. This task focuses on developing a proactive framework for regularly monitoring and maintaining the security posture of an organization's OT systems.

Continuous Monitoring Strategy Key Elements

- **Integration with Risk Management:** The strategy is integrated efficiently into the organization's overall risk management projects, ensuring a consistent approach to enterprise risk.

- **Dynamic Approach:** The strategy is customized to the changing nature of security threats and emphasizes responsiveness to changes in system settings and operational procedures.

- **Comprehensive Measures:** It addresses and adapts to evolving security threats through a combination of periodic reviews, real-time analytics, and proactive mitigation activities.

Objectives of Continuous Monitoring

The primary purpose of establishing a continuous monitoring approach is to maintain and improve the security defenses of OT systems in the face of continually changing threats and advancements in technology.

The key objectives include:

- **Adaptability:** The strategy is intended to develop in response to new threats, technical advancements, and changes in operational procedures, ensuring that the system's security measures remain effective and up to date.

- **Resilience:** By predicting possible risks and applying preventative actions, the approach seeks to strengthen the system's ability to resist and recover from security incidents.

- **Core Value Preservation:** Continuous monitoring is critical for ensuring that the OT system constantly adheres to the values of integrity, confidentiality, and availability, regardless of external forces or internal changes.

Task S-5 focuses on building a continuous monitoring plan to preserve and sustain operational technology systems. Organizations that use an adaptable and integrated approach to monitoring could ensure that their OT systems are not only safeguarded against current risks but also well-prepared to tackle future problems. This plan, in line with NIST SP 800-82, demonstrates the significance of awareness and adaptation in the ever-changing world of OT cybersecurity.

6.31 IMPLEMENT

The "Implement" phase of the Risk Management Framework (RMF) represents an important transformation from theoretical planning to actual action inside an organization's operational technology (OT) systems. This stage is dedicated to implementing the previously specified security controls and measures, with a concentration on deploying or updating these controls in new and existing systems.

Key Components in the Implementation Stage

- **Installation of Physical Safeguards:** Includes installing physical safeguards such as biometrics or obstacles to prevent unwanted access.

- **Configuration of Technical Safeguards:** Activities include the installation of firewalls, intrusion detection systems, encryption protocols, and other technical steps to safeguard the system's integrity and confidentiality.

- **Adoption of Administrative Safeguards:** Developing and implementing policies, processes, and training programs to strengthen the organization's security infrastructure and awareness.

Approach to Implementation

- **New Systems:** This step is an essential turning point before launch, verifying that all security measures are integrated and operational.

- **Existing Systems:** Maintenance or downtime planning may be required as part of the installation process, with a priority on minimizing operating disruptions while installing new controls.

Challenges and Compliance

Implementing security controls is a complicated process that frequently necessitates coordination across several functional teams to ensure that the measures efficiently minimize threats without impacting the system's functionality.

- **Objective:** To develop a balanced cybersecurity posture that is consistent with the organization's overall risk management strategy, assuring the protection of critical infrastructure components.

Verification and Documentation

The rigorous testing and recording of each control's efficacy are critical throughout the deployment phase. This not only validates the effective implementation of the security measures but also allows for continuing monitoring and compliance checks, creating the framework for continual development of the security posture.

The "Implement" phase is an important turning point in the RMF, where strategic planning meets actual execution. Organizations may dramatically improve their cybersecurity by carefully establishing, setting, and evaluating security measures inside OT systems. This phase necessitates careful consideration of detail, cross-departmental collaboration, and a persistent commitment to the organization's overall risk management goals, all of which ensure the long-term security and stability of operating technology.

6.32 TASK I-1: CONTROL IMPLEMENTATION

Task I-1, which focuses on "Implementation of Controls," underlines the importance of incorporating security measures into operational technology (OT) systems. This work ensures that security upgrades are integrated into the fundamental structure of ordinary system maintenance and operation, increasing the system's ability to adapt to possible attacks while preserving its performance and functionality. Integrating security procedures into normal maintenance is necessary for making robust structures without creating vulnerabilities or interruptions.

Key Components of Control Implementation

Software Upgrades for Security Enhancement: Regular software upgrades are necessary for strengthening the system's defenses against evolving cyber threats, necessitating smart planning to reduce downtime in key infrastructure.

- **Enhanced Physical Security:** Improving physical access controls to prevent unwanted entrance or tampering with vital operational technology components.

- **Configuration Changes for Increased Security:** Modifying system configurations to increase security layers, which may include network segmentation, stronger authentication methods, and strict access limits.

Challenges in OT Systems:

- **Operational Continuity:** Since OT systems are essential and cannot be taken offline for upgrades or alterations, establishing security measures requires new solutions for continuous operation.

- **Creativity in Security Solutions**: In some cases, innovative, temporary security techniques may be required to offer urgent protection until more complete solutions can be installed without compromising system availability.

Goal of Task I-1

The major goal of this work is to protect OT systems from cyber attacks by including strong security measures in their operations. This requires careful planning and execution to strike a fine balance between improving security and preserving system performance and dependability.

The successful deployment of security measures inside OT systems is a complicated yet critical task that demands careful consideration, creativeness, and in-depth knowledge of the system's operating requirements. Task I-1 highlights the need to incorporate security measures into the fabric of system maintenance and operation to create a stronger posture against cyber-attacks while assuring the continuous operation of key infrastructure components. This strategy not only improves the security posture, but also coincides with the larger goals of ensuring system integrity, availability, and performance in the face of emerging cyber threats.

6.33 TASK I-2: UPDATE CONTROL IMPLEMENTATION INFORMATION

Task I-2, "Update Control Implementation Information," is important for keeping an accurate and complete record of the security posture of operational technology (OT) systems. This activity includes recording modifications, updates, and new discoveries that arise when security measures are added and modified throughout the system.

Task I-2's Core Components

- **Maintenance of Security Records:** Includes maintaining security records that reflect current system setups and controls.

- **Documentation of Challenges and Solutions:** Documenting issues encountered during the implementation of security measures, how these obstacles were handled, and efforts made to improve security standards.

- **Continuous Optimization:** Updating implementation knowledge allows for continual refining of security techniques, resulting in more efficient resolution of future concerns.

Objectives of Task I-2

- **Accuracy in Security Documentation:** Aims to ensure accurate and thorough security documentation by maintaining an extensive log of setups, upgrades, and problem-solving activities.
- **Streamlined Troubleshooting:** Maintaining an up-to-date security implementation record makes it easier to diagnose and resolve future security events, allowing for faster and more effective responses.
- **Audit and Evaluation Readiness:** A well-maintained security document helps the firm prepare for audits and evaluations, exhibiting a proactive attitude to cybersecurity management.
- **Dynamic Response to Changes:** Making security documentation adaptive, enabling for fast updates in response to new threats or system changes.
- **Supporting Security Culture:** Encouraging openness and informed decision-making in security management by maintaining clear and accurate records of security measures and their effectiveness.

Task I-2 is essential in the continuing management of security in OT systems, underlining the significance of accurate and dynamic documentation of control implementation. Organizations may improve their cybersecurity posture, accelerate problem-solving efforts, and assure preparation for audits and assessments by maintaining a complete and up-to-date record of security changes, issues faced, and solutions implemented. This activity promotes a culture of continuous improvement and informed decision-making in cybersecurity management, which is critical for ensuring the integrity and resilience of OT systems in the face of emerging threats.

6.34 ASSESS

The "Assess" step of the Risk Management Framework (RMF) plays an important role in the OT security lifecycle. It offers enterprises an important opportunity to properly assess the effectiveness of their security procedures. This phase focuses on ensuring that security measures not only exist but also effectively minimize threats.

Key Activities in the Assess Phase

- **Assessment Methods:** During the assessment phase, organizations use various assessment methods such as audits, penetration testing, and security reviews to ensure that security measures are properly installed and working.

- **Evidence Gathering:** Evidence collection occurs through extensive testing and observation to prove the presence and operational efficiency of security measures.

- **Evidence Analysis:** This stage comprises a thorough evaluation of the acquired evidence to determine the effectiveness of the established controls and identify any shortcomings.

- **Documentation of Results:** The assessment results are properly documented. This documentation is an important resource for both current and future security evaluations.

Objectives of the Assess Phase

- **Verification of Control Effectiveness:** Aims to verify the effectiveness of security controls and ensure they fit with organizational policies.

- **Identification of Security Gaps:** Using this evaluation approach, businesses may identify areas where security measures may be absent or underperforming, giving a foundation for future improvements.

- **Informed Decision-Making:** The information gathered from the evaluation allows for educated decisions about improving or adjusting security measures.

- **Continuous Security Improvement:** Rather than being a one-time study, the "Assess" step is part of an evolutionary process for maintaining and improving system security over time.

The "Assess" step is essential for providing the robustness and tolerance of OT systems to cybersecurity attacks. By systematically analyzing the performance of security procedures, companies may discover areas for improvement, improving their overall security posture. This phase promotes a culture of continual improvement and careful monitoring, which is important for safeguarding critical operating technology.

6.35 TASK A-1: ASSESSOR SELECTION

The selection of assessors, known as Task A-1, initiates the Risk Management Framework's (RMF) assessment process for Operational Technology (OT) systems. This stage is basic and important to the whole process, as it aims to designate an adept assessment team or an independent assessor with the necessary competence to comprehensively examine the security policies and procedures established inside operational systems.

Criteria for Assessor Selection:

- **Expertise in Cybersecurity and OT Systems:** Assessors must have a thorough awareness of cybersecurity concepts, as well as particular knowledge of the unique features of OT systems. This involves understanding the differences in architecture, operational details, and risk landscapes between OT and typical IT settings.

- **Comprehensive Skill Set:** Ideal applicants for the assessment team should have a diverse set of skills, including system security, industrial control system competence, network design knowledge, and a thorough understanding of risk management methods.

- **Impartiality and Objectivity:** Assessors must maintain a neutral attitude, free of any conflicts of interest. Their capacity to conduct fair and objective evaluations is critical to the validity of the assessment process.

Objectives for Assessor Selection

- **Effective Evaluation of Security Controls:** The importance of selecting skilled assessors arises from their ability to properly evaluate the efficacy of security measures inside OT systems, identifying their effectiveness in minimizing prevalent risks and alignment with the organization's broader risk management goals.

- **System Compliance and Security:** Through accurate investigation, assessors help to strengthen OT systems' security posture, ensure compliance with key standards and guidelines, and identify opportunities for improvement.

- **Guiding Risk Management Efforts:** The insights gained from the assessment process, guided by experienced assessors, serve as a compass for navigating subsequent risk management actions inside the RMF, forming plans for improved system security.

Task A-1 highlights the need for a thoughtful and identifying approach to assessor selection, which is essential to the success of the RMF's OT system evaluation phase. Organizations may strengthen their protection against changing cybersecurity threats by putting experience, objectivity, and an in-depth knowledge of OT system complexities first.

6.36 TASK A-2: ASSESSMENT PLAN

The "Assessment Plan," referred to as Task A-2 within the Risk Management Framework (RMF), is an essential stage in assessing the security framework of Operational Technology (OT) systems. This phase is essential, laying the groundwork for a thorough evaluation of the security measures' efficiency and dependability.

Key Components of the Assessment Plan

- **Comprehensive Detailing:** The strategy requires a detailed overview that includes the security measures to be examined, the approach and resources to be used, the schedule for execution, and the assignment of particular roles to team members.

- **Scope and Objectives:** It defines the scope of the assessment and articulates specific objectives, offering a road map for the assessment team to evaluate the security framework's maturity and strength.

- **Approval and Readiness:** Before execution, management reviews and approves the assessment plan, demonstrating their commitment to meeting the defined cybersecurity goals.

Objectives for Creating an Assessment Plan

- **Managing the Assessment Process:** The assessment plan serves as a strategic roadmap, ensuring that all relevant security measures are inspected using the most appropriate techniques and methods.

- **Establishing Standards and Expectations**: The strategy outlines the criteria and benchmarks against which the security framework will be tested, as well as the assessment's expected outcomes.

- **Facilitating Organizational Readiness:** By obtaining management approval, the assessment plan demonstrates the organization's readiness to conduct a full examination of its cybersecurity posture, allocating resources and focusing on validating the system's security integrity.

Task A-2, developing an Assessment Plan, is crucial for providing the basis for a systematic and comprehensive examination of an organization's OT security architecture. The plan serves as a guide document for the assessment team, including the scope, techniques, dates, and responsibilities. This ensures a disciplined approach to evaluating the security measures in place. With management's approval, the business demonstrates its willingness to critically examine and improve its cybersecurity maturity, demonstrating its commitment to protecting its operational technology systems.

6.37 Task A-3: Control Assessment

Task A-3, named "Control Assessments," has significance to the Risk Management Framework (RMF) since it conducts in-depth evaluations of security controls in Operational Technology (OT) systems. This work is intended to extensively test each control to ensure that it is effective in minimizing risks.

Control Assessment Key Elements:

- **Methodological Approach:** Uses a variety of assessment techniques, including findings from past assessments and automated systems, to assure accuracy and reduce operational disturbance.

- **Operational Integrity:** Emphasizes simple methods for preserving the functionality of OT systems, acknowledging the importance of these systems to corporate objectives.

- **Automation and Precision:** Emphasizes the use of automated technologies to decrease human error and assure the continued operation of OT systems.

Control assessment Objectives

- **Effectiveness Evaluation:** Includes evaluating the efficiency of the operation of security measures and their contribution to risk management strategy.

- **Risk Reduction Verification:** Determines the extent to which security controls reduce risks within the OT framework.

- **Documentation and Future Planning:** Accurately document control failures to help create future security measures and reassessments.

The Importance of Control Assessments in OT Security

- **Enhanced Security Posture**: Protects OT systems from both existing and future threats, ensuring the integrity and availability of essential operations.

- **Adaptation and Resilience:** By precisely recognizing and recording control failures, Task A-3 establishes the platform for continual development in the OT security architecture, enabling adaptation to emerging threats.

Task A-3, Control Assessments, is an essential component of the RMF that protects the security and dependability of operational technology systems. Through thorough examination and documentation, it ensures that security measures are successfully decreasing risks, hence improving the organization's overall security posture. This work underlines the significance of a targeted, simple approach to security assessments to ensure the operational continuity and resilience of OT systems.

6.38 TASK A-4: ASSESSMENT REPORTS

Task A-4 includes the preparation of an assessment report, which is a significant document that combines the findings from the security controls evaluation phase of the Risk Management Framework. This report provides a thorough record of the effectiveness, shortcomings, and results of tested controls, laying the groundwork for future compliance and improvement initiatives within the company.

Functions of the Assessment Report

- **Documentation:** Serves as a repository for information on the performance and efficiency of security controls, including where and how effectively they work.

- **Accountability:** Clearly defines the organization's duties and functions, indicating who manages which security controls.

- **Decision-Making:** Informs organizational choices, particularly at the executive level, by giving actionable insights and suggestions based on assessment results.

- **Improvement Blueprint:** Provides prescriptive suggestions for correcting identified shortcomings or gaps, and serves as a framework for improving the organization's security posture.

- **Compliance Assurance:** Indicates the organization's commitment to implementing strong security measures and ensuring openness to its operations.

Importance of the Report

The assessment report plays an essential role in filling the gap between security evaluations and practical recommendations. It is important for auditors and regulatory agencies with a thorough understanding of the organization's security structure, to ensure that all stakeholders are aware of the existing security posture and planned changes.

Creating the Report: Balancing Art and Science

Creating a successful evaluation report necessitates an advanced strategy that blends thorough detail with strategic interpretation. The report should be designed to provide clear, instructive insights while also allowing for practical implementations of its suggestions. The goal is to develop a document that is both instructive and useful in directing the company to a more secure and compliant future.

Task A-4, which focuses on the creation of assessment reports, is an important stage in the Risk Management Framework that combines the findings of security control evaluations into an organized and actionable document. This report has significance for documenting existing security measures, increasing accountability, directing decision-making, and preparing for future improvements. It guarantees that the firm remains dedicated to improving its security posture while adhering to applicable standards and laws.

6.39 TASK A-5: REMEDIATION ACTIONS

Task A-5, which focuses on Remediation Actions, is essential for improving a system's security defenses. This duty goes beyond simple fixes; it stresses the deployment of proactive procedures aimed at preventing future vulnerabilities. The process integrates strategic planning and execution to effectively handle and reduce risks, ensuring the company's adaptability to possible threats.

Steps in Remediation Actions

- **Prioritization:** Begin by addressing the vulnerabilities with the highest risk, weighing the chance of exploitation against the possible consequences. This method aids in the best allocation of resources by focusing on minimizing the most significant risks first.

- **Creating Comprehensive Solutions:** Solutions might range from software patching and upgrading encryption standards to enhancing access restrictions and changing operational practices. The goal is to not just address present concerns but also to strengthen the system's overall security posture.

- **Mindful Implementation:** Interventions should be executed with a keen understanding of the system's operating requirements. The major goal is to strengthen security measures while preserving the system's operation and safety regulations.

- **Documentation:** Explain the reasoning for the chosen corrective activities, the implementation process, and any revisions. This record is a significant resource for future security planning and initiatives.

- **Verification:** After implementation, it is critical to assess the effectiveness of the remedial actions. Ensure that these activities did not introduce new vulnerabilities and that they strengthened the system's integrity and operating efficiency.

The goal of Task A-5 is to strike a balance between improving system security and maintaining operational capabilities. This balance is important for ensuring that security upgrades are not compromising system performance or the organization's ability to meet its goals. Organizations may address vulnerabilities systematically by following the procedures listed below, protecting their systems from existing and future security threats while maintaining operational excellence.

6.40 TASK A-6: PLAN OF ACTION AND MILESTONES

Task A-6, referred to as the "Plan of Action and Milestones," provides an in-depth direction for fixing discovered security or privacy vulnerabilities in the Operational Technology (OT) framework. This strategic plan plays an important role in directing companies through the process of addressing problems identified during the evaluation phase.

Components of the Plan

- **Remediation Strategies:** The plan includes specific remediation strategies for each identified risk, including enhanced technology, updated processes, and policy modifications as needed.

- **Defined Timelines:** Sets out clear implementation timelines, deadlines, and critical milestones to guarantee an organized and timely resolution.

- **Resource Allocation:** Identifies the people and technology resources that will be used to effectively execute remediation efforts.

- **Risk Prioritization:** Points out the importance of addressing certain risks above others depending on their potential effect, ensuring that significant vulnerabilities are prioritized.

- **Operational Considerations:** Ensures that maintenance activities do not disrupt critical functions while adhering to the operating schedules of the OT systems.

- **Ongoing Evaluation and Revision:** Highlights the plan's adaptable character, which requires regular evaluations and changes to stay successful over time.

The Plan of Action and Milestones are important for moving from the evaluation phase to taking specific measures to improve the security posture of OT systems. It attempts not only to address present vulnerabilities but also to harden the system against future attacks, all while ensuring the operational continuity required in OT contexts. This paper demonstrates the organization's dedication to proactive security management, which ensures an efficient and secure operational technology landscape.

6.41 AUTHORIZE

The "Authorize" step of the Risk Management Framework (RMF) is an important phase in which the organization's leadership assesses and makes critical choices about a system's operational preparedness based on its security posture. This phase is led by a selected senior official known as the Authorizing Official (AO), who is responsible for examining the system's security measures and deciding whether it will be operational.

Key Activities of the Authorization Process

- **Documentation Review:** The AO thoroughly evaluates the security package, which includes the system description, detected vulnerabilities, assessment results, and enhancement plans.

- **Understanding of Residual Risk:** To determine the risk level that the company is willing to tolerate, a thorough evaluation of residual risk—that is, the risk that remains after important controls have been implemented is accomplished.

- **Risk-Based Decision Making:** The AO determines if the system's security state matches the organization's risk tolerance levels, resulting in a conclusion on whether the system can be operational, requires more remediation, or is judged too high-risk for deployment.

- **Issuance of Authorization to Operate (ATO):** Issuance is issued following a positive decision, which may include conditions, a validity duration, or a review schedule.

The authorization procedure demonstrates the organization's commitment to carefully examining a system's security features. It represents the transition from assessment to approval, ensuring that only systems that fulfill the stated risk criteria are permitted to function. This stage emphasizes the need for ongoing evaluation and the need to adjust authorizations in response to evolving risks and vulnerabilities, hence ensuring the organization's resilience and security.

6.42 TASK R-1: AUTHORIZATION PACKAGE

The Authorization Package, specified in Task R-1 of the Risk Management Framework (RMF), is essential for determining a system's operational validity. It gathers all of the required information to make sure that the system's functioning is secure.

Components of the Authorization Package

- **System Documentation:** Outlines the system's architecture, data flows, functionality, and security mechanisms. This paper is essential for understanding the system's design and security infrastructure.

- **Security Assessment Report:** This document summarizes the findings of security assessments, including test results, the effectiveness of security measures against possible threats, and the system's operational resilience.

- **Plan of Action and Milestones (POA&M):** A strategy document based on previous evaluations that outlines essential corrective measures and deadlines. The POA&M has significance for monitoring progress in addressing identified risks.

- **Risk Assessment Report:** Analyzes residual risks following the deployment of security measures, providing a thorough risk profile for the system. This study is useful for analyzing the possible effect of unsolved security concerns.

- **Supporting Documentation:** Includes extra resources that provide credibility to the system's security statements, such as policies, processes, and records of previous permission decisions. These papers are critical for determining if the system complies with established security requirements and corporate rules.

The creation and maintenance of a correct, up-to-date Authorization Package is important. It requires great attention to detail to ensure that it matches the organization's risk tolerance and regulatory compliance. The package helps the Authorizing Official (AO) or senior management to make intelligent decisions about the system's deployment while balancing operational requirements with the security landscape. This decision-making process seeks a positive outcome in which the system is used best within its assigned operational context.

6.43 TASK R-2: RISK ANALYSIS AND DETERMINATION

Task R-2 in the Risk Management Framework (RMF) is an essential task known as "Risk Analysis and Determination". This assignment requires the Authorizing Official (AO) to conduct a critical assessment of the system's risk posture using a full and comprehensive Authorization Package.

Key Components of Risk Assessment and Determination

- **Comprehensive Evaluation:** The AO undertakes a thorough examination of the system's risk state, informed by the precise information provided in the Authorization Package. This review examines the effectiveness of deployed security measures and identifies any remaining threats.

- **Alignment with Organizational Policies:** The risk status is compared to the organization's established risk management policies. The purpose is to assess whether the system's security posture is compatible with the organization's predetermined risk criteria.

- **Decision Making:** The AO serves as a gatekeeper, determining if the present system configuration fulfills the organization's risk acceptance requirements or whether further controls are required to reduce detected risks.

- **Balancing Security and Operational Needs:** This stage highlights the significance of preserving the system's operational requirements while pursuing optimal security. The balance between security measures and system functioning is important.

- **Risk Projection:** Future security issues are forecasted using existing data and information security trends. This forward-thinking strategy assists in preparing the system to deal with emerging risks.

Ensuring System Readiness Task R-2 ensures that the system if deployed, does not represent a significant threat to organizational operations and assets. The AO assesses the system's operational readiness or the need for improved security measures by carefully analyzing risk against organizational standards and future forecasts. This method demonstrates the RMF's dynamic character, expertly moving between current security requirements and predicting future risks.

6.44 TASK R-3: RISK RESPONSE

Task R-3, also known as "Risk Response," is a significant step in management's strategy for handling risks in Operational Technology (OT) systems. This stage goes beyond initial risk assessment to actively identify and reduce risks depending on their severity and the seriousness of possible threats.

Key Components of Risk Response

- **Strategic Planning:** The development of strategic plans suited to individual risks serves as the foundation for risk response. This planning is critical, especially given the central role of OT systems in organizational operations.

- **Actionable Measures:** These might include deploying fixes to vulnerabilities, changing operating procedures, or introducing new security measures. The objective is to quickly neutralize or minimize risks to avoid operational interruptions or harm.

- **Adaptability:** It is an important feature of risk response because it allows for quick adaptation to shifting threats. This adaptable strategy ensures that OT systems can respond to new problems while providing adequate protection against any security breaches.

- **Systematic Problem Solving:** Responses to recognized risks are carried out using precise and systematic methods, ensuring that solutions directly address the identified weaknesses and threats.

Importance of OT System Protection

- **Core of Organizational Processes**: Organizational processes rely heavily on OT systems, highlighting the importance of protecting them. Protecting these systems from potential attacks is essential for ensuring operational integrity and continuity.

- **Minimizing Harm:** Effective risk response techniques attempt to reduce potential harm and avoid operational failures. Organizations may protect their assets and staff by responding quickly to vulnerabilities.

Goal of Risk Response

- **Sustaining Operations:** Task R-3 is to protect the security and efficiency of OT systems, preventing security threats from disrupting the organization's core activities.

- **Organizational Safety:** By carefully implementing risk response mechanisms, businesses want to safeguard not just operating technology, but also the safety of their surroundings and workers from the consequences of security events.

Task R-3 outlines a proactive strategy for controlling risks in OT systems, underlining the importance of planned, flexible, and systematic responses to possible threats. Organizations may maintain operational resilience and continue to conduct key functions without interruption by prioritizing OT system protection. This work highlights the need for a strong risk management approach in protecting the core of organizational operations from growing security threats.

6.45 TASK R-4: AUTHORIZATION DECISION

Task R-4, designated "Authorization Decision," is a critical stage within the Risk Management Framework that requires the direct engagement of an Authorizing Official (AO). This phase concludes a series of in-depth examinations, providing several options for risk mitigation before reaching this key point.

Key Aspects of the Authorization Decision

- **Comprehensive Review:** The Authorization Decision involves a thorough evaluation of system documentation, including risk assessments and security measures, within the context of operational technology (OT).

- **Risk Evaluation:** Central to this role is the AO's assessment of whether the existing safeguards have reduced risks to an acceptable level, allowing the OT system to run securely and effectively.

- **Collaborative Problem Solving:** When residual risks exceed the organization's tolerance level, the AO works with the security team to develop suitable solutions specific to the OT context. This might involve additional protections, contingency preparations, or taking some risks with full knowledge of the potential consequences.

The Balance of Authorization Decision

- **Operational vs. Security Needs:** The authorization decision strikes a delicate balance between the requirement to sustain uninterrupted operations and the need to conform to security standards.

- **Ongoing Commitment:** Beyond a single ruling, the decision demonstrates a commitment to ongoing security management, which ensures the OT system's adaptability to emerging threats.

Task R-4 underlines the Authorization Decision's essential function in crossing the fine line between operational goals and security needs in the Operational Technology ecosystem. By making enlightened judgments, AOs not only ensure safe and efficient system operations but also demonstrate their dedication to maintaining the highest security management standards. This approach is critical for preserving the integrity of OT systems and assuring their continuing protection against emerging threats.

6.46 TASK R-5: AUTHORIZATION REPORTING

Task R-5, known as "Authorization Reporting," underlines the need for open communication in cybersecurity management. This duty in the Risk Management Framework focuses on conveying the results of authorization decisions to key stakeholders within the company.

Core Objectives of Authorization Reporting

- **Stakeholder Communication:** Authorization Reporting aims to communicate the cybersecurity status of OT systems to department leaders, security chiefs, and top executives. This includes identifying vulnerabilities, and threats, proposed corrective actions, and authorization decisions.

- **Comprehensive Coverage:** The report should cover the whole review process, including decision rationales and the consequences for organizational operations, to ensure a thorough knowledge of cybersecurity measures and outcomes.

- **Future Reference:** Serves as a crucial record for future audits, policy refinement, and proof in the case of a security breach, demonstrating the history of risk management choices and actions taken.

Functions of Authorization Reporting

- **Notification and Demonstration:** It not only aims to keep key employees informed, but it also demonstrates the organization's commitment to upholding strong security standards.

- **Audit and Policy Refinement:** Provides a foundation for examining and enhancing security policies and procedures using recorded results and choices.

- **Breach Preparedness:** In the event of a security incident, the report provides useful insights into the procedures taken to mitigate risks, assisting with reaction and recovery activities.

Task R-5 highlights the need for good communication in cybersecurity management under the Operational Technology framework. Authorization Reporting is essential in ensuring that all relevant parties are aware of the cybersecurity posture, allowing for informed decision-making and demonstrating the organization's commitment to protecting its OT systems from emerging threats. Organizations may improve their cybersecurity strategy, prepare for future audits, and strengthen their defensive systems against possible intrusions by producing extensive and easily available reports.

6.47 MONITOR

The Monitoring phase, a key component of the Risk Management Framework, indicates a continuing commitment to an organization's cybersecurity. Unlike a final phase, it marks the start of a proactive and ongoing process aimed at protecting the organization's cybersecurity health in the face of new threats and operational shifts.

Core Practices for Continuous Monitoring

- **System Log Reviews:** Involves a thorough examination of system logs for anomalies or evidence of security events.

- **Incident Detection:** Actively seeking for and responding to security incidents as they occur.

- **Pattern Analysis:** Using analytics to detect odd activity patterns that might signal a security concern.

- **Control Reassessment:** This is the process of reviewing the effectiveness of imposed security measures regularly to verify they are still operating properly.

Key Objectives of Continuous Monitoring

- **Adaptation to Emerging Threats:** Staying up to date on emerging threats and developments in technology that may demand security control upgrades.

- **Proactive Security Measures:** Includes anticipating future security threats and modifying procedures accordingly to ensure system integrity.

- **Informed Decision-Making:** Using monitoring data to improve risk response methods and management measures.

Importance of Real-time Monitoring

Real-time monitoring allows for the rapid response to and mitigation of security risks, ensuring system operational resilience and integrity. It allows the security team to:

- **Adjust Protection Strategies:** Tailoring security measures to effectively combat detected threats.

- **Efficient Incident Response:** Requires establishing fast and efficient responses to security issues.

- **Risk Management:** Ensuring that organizational threats are kept within acceptable limits as established by risk management guidelines.

The monitoring phase is essential to ensure the continuing cybersecurity of operational technology systems. Organizations can ensure their resilience against the ever-changing cyber threat landscape by including continuous and thorough monitoring operations in their cybersecurity strategy. This phase not only protects the organization's technology assets but also helps it achieve its overall goals by maintaining the necessary levels of system security and integrity.

6.48 TASK M-1: CHECKING SYSTEM AND ENVIRONMENT CHANGES

Task M-1 of the Risk Management Framework's Monitoring phase highlights the importance of continuous monitoring for any changes in the Operational Technology (OT) environment. This duty relies on the careful monitoring and study of the technical environment, particularly systems connected to major industrial processes, to ensure their security and dependability.

Core Actions for Monitoring Changes

- **Routine Surveillance:** Consistent monitoring to detect changes in the system or its surroundings that may compromise security.

- **Recording Alterations:** Alterations should be carefully documented, whether they be software upgrades, hardware changes, user access adjustments, or variations in the system's physical surroundings.

- **Detecting Irregularities:** Identifying deviations from routine activities that might indicate a security issue.

Consistent Monitoring Objectives

- **Awareness:** Maintaining a continual understanding of the system's condition to detect any changes that might represent a security risk.

- **Proactive Response:** Positioning the company to resolve vulnerabilities quickly, reducing the likelihood of exploitation by hostile actors.

- **Reliability and Accessibility:** Ensuring that systems connected to important machinery are secure, accessible, and dependable, which is critical in OT contexts.

Importance of Task M1

Task M-1 is critical to maintaining the operational integrity and security of OT systems. Implementing a proactive monitoring approach allows firms to:

- **Safeguard Operations:** Protect the systems from possible threats and weaknesses.

- **Maintain Operational Continuity:** Make certain that any system modifications do not disrupt the continuous and dependable operation of important processes.

- **Improved Risk Management:** Incorporate all identified changes into the overall risk assessment and management plan, ensuring that security measures grow in parallel with system and environmental changes.

Task M-1 confirms businesses' commitment to ensuring the security, safety, and dependability of their operational technology systems. Constant monitoring of system and environmental changes is not just a cybersecurity need; it is also essential to ensuring the efficiency and reliability of operations in OT environments. This duty is critical to the organization's proactive risk management and demonstrates its commitment to a safe and robust operating structure.

6.49 TASK M-2: ONGOING ASSESSMENT

In the Risk Management Framework, Task M-2 highlights the importance of continual evaluations during the monitoring phase. This role assures systematic and continual reviews of security policies and procedures inside an organization's operational framework, which is essential to ensuring the security integrity of operational technology (OT) systems.

Core Components of Ongoing Assessments

- **Scheduled and Unscheduled Reviews:** Uses both routine recertifications and spontaneous assessments to react to the changing security situation.

- **Post-Implementation Evaluations:** Conducts detailed assessments of security measures after they are implemented to ensure their efficacy and alignment with the intended security objectives.

- **Security Mechanism Validation:** Ensures that evaluations are completed in a way that is not detrimental to system security, hence maintaining the system's operational integrity.

Importance of Task M-2

Task M-2 is critical for the continued security and operational dependability of OT systems by:

- **Ensuring System Security:** Validates the ongoing efficacy of security policies and procedures in the face of a shifting threat landscape.

- **Promoting Adaptive Security Measures:** Allows for rapid adaptation to operational changes and emerging threats, ensuring that security measures are both reactive and proactive.

- **Facilitating Strategic Decision-Making:** Serves as a foundation for intelligent choices about security policy changes and upgrades.

Task M-2 underlines the importance of continuous awareness and assessment in the OT environment. Organizations may ensure that their OT systems are protected against existing and future risks by conducting systematic continuous evaluations, which secure important operational processes. This duty not only confirms the organization's commitment to security but also assures that its OT systems perform effectively and reliably within an acceptable risk threshold, which is consistent with the Risk Management Framework's overall goals.

6.50 TASK M-3: ONGOING RISK RESPONSE

Task M-3, known as "Ongoing Risk Response," highlights the essential significance of continuous awareness and reactivity in IT and OT environments. This role focuses on the capacity to quickly discover, analyze, and respond to signals of possible security risks, preserving the system's integrity and operational continuity.

Key Elements of Ongoing Risk Response

- **Alert Monitoring:** Ongoing risk response includes alert monitoring for suspicious actions or irregularities that may pose security issues.

- **Risk assessment:** This is a quick examination of warnings to determine the amount of threat and related risk to the system's security posture.

- **Immediate Action:** Implementing immediate actions to reduce recognized threats. Actions may include improving security protocols, applying required updates to vulnerabilities, or even partly shutting down systems to prevent prospective intrusions.

Objectives of Active Risk Response

- **Rapid Identification and Neutralization:** Ensures that emergent threats are detected and mitigated as soon as possible, minimizing system damage.

- **Defensive Integrity Preservation:** Ensures that the system's security protections perform properly, preventing breaches and unwanted access.

- **Enhanced System Resilience:** Increases the system's capacity to withstand present and future security threats, hence improving its overall defense mechanism.

Importance of Task M-3

The completion of Task M-3 is essential for:

- **Maintaining Operational Security:** Ensures that all possible risks are detected and addressed immediately to keep IT and OT systems secure against developing threats.

- **System Reliability:** Ensures that systems are operational and dependable by preventing security breaches that might interrupt important processes.

- **Building Defensive Capacity:** Helps to establish a stronger security posture capable of responding to and recovering from security incidents.

Task M-3 is a fundamental component of the Risk Management Framework, highlighting the necessity for a continuing, proactive approach to risk management in operational technology systems. Organizations can make sure that their IT and OT systems stay safe against immediate threats while also being better positioned to manage future security issues by creating an atmosphere in which risks are quickly detected and handled. This continual risk response plan is crucial for ensuring the integrity, availability, and dependability of essential operating systems.

6.51 TASK M-4: AUTHORIZATION PACKAGE UPDATES

Task M-4, which focuses on frequent changes to authorization documents, is an important component in the security management of operational technology (OT) systems throughout their entire existence. This work is crucial for adding the most recent insights and results obtained from continuous system monitoring into the permission package.

Key Components of Authorization Package Updates

- **Change in Documentation:** Every change in the system is captured and recorded, including trends in threat detection, newly discovered vulnerabilities, and security measure upgrades.

- **Dynamic Documentation:** Highlights the significance of making the authorization package as adaptive and responsive as the OT systems it is intended to protect.

- **Regular Updates:** Ensures that the documentation is revised regularly with the most up-to-date and correct information, allowing for more informed decisions.

Objectives of Updating the Authorization Package

- **Informed Decision Making:** Provides decision-makers with up-to-date information, allowing them to maintain a strong security posture.

- **Proactive Risk Management:** Encourages a proactive approach to risk management by ensuring that the business is constantly ready to respond to new threats and vulnerabilities as they arise.

- **Effective Communication:** Improves communication within the organization by informing all stakeholders on the current security state and the efficacy of applied measures.

Importance of Task M-4

The completion of Task M-4 is essential for:

- **Maintaining System Security:** Keeps the OT systems' security mechanisms up to date with the newest threat landscape and technical breakthroughs.

- **Supporting Continuous Improvement:** Makes it easier to enhance security procedures by laying the groundwork for regular reviews and adjustments to security strategy.

- **Regulatory Compliance:** Assists in maintaining the organization's compliance with key security standards and regulations by documenting all essential information and activities.

Task M-4 underlines the importance of updating the authorization package for OT systems as part of an overall risk management plan. Organizations may improve risk management, make informed choices, and preserve the integrity and adaptability of their operational technology systems by ensuring that the documentation appropriately represents the current status of the system's security posture. This work highlights the need for a dynamic and proactive approach to documentation and risk management, confirming the organization's commitment to operating in a safe environment.

6.52 TASK M-5: SECURITY AND PRIVACY REPORTING

Task M-5 covers the essential task of preparing and providing security and privacy reports to top management in a business. This activity is essential for providing a clear and accessible assessment of existing security and privacy practices, underlining the effectiveness of implemented measures, identifying any major privacy problems, and verifying compliance with legal and regulatory requirements.

Fundamentals of Security and Privacy Reporting

- **Comprehensive Overview:** Provides a comprehensive overview of the organization's security and privacy landscape, with an emphasis on the effectiveness of security measures and privacy concerns.

- **Management Briefing:** Designed to be transparent and straightforward, senior management can understand the key features of the security and privacy posture without being overwhelmed by excessive detail.

- **Actionable insights:** The reports are designed to help decision-makers prioritize security and privacy projects, spend resources efficiently, and strengthen the organization's cybersecurity defenses.

Objectives of Security and Privacy Reporting

- **Effective Decision Making:** Enables top management to make well-informed choices about security and privacy strategies, budget allocation, and project priority.

- **Resource allocation:** Assists in the effective allocation of resources to areas that require the greatest development or reinforcement, ensuring that existing assets are used optimally to increase security and privacy.

- **Regulatory Compliance:** Ensures that the organization continues to comply with applicable legal and regulatory standards, avoiding potential penalties and punishments.

Importance of Task M-5

- **Maintaining Organizational Accountability:** Ensures that top management is well-informed and accountable for the organization's security and privacy posture, establishing a proactive risk management culture.

- **Anticipating Security Risks:** Enables executives to anticipate and manage possible security risks before they occur, hence increasing the organization's overall resilience.

- **Upholding Privacy Standards:** Ensures that privacy problems are properly managed and resolved, hence protecting the organization's reputation and consumer confidence.

Task M-5 addresses the importance of regular and transparent communication about security and privacy issues with the organization's senior management. These reports are essential for informed decision-making, effective resource allocation, and proactive risk management strategies because they provide a clear yet comprehensive picture of the security and privacy situation. Finally, Security and Privacy Reporting is an essential component of a strong operational technology system security architecture, demonstrating the organization's commitment to protecting its assets, data, and reputation.

6.53 TASK M-6: ONGOING AUTHORISATION

Task M-6, also known as "Ongoing Authorization," is crucial for ensuring that organizational processes operate with ongoing permission. This activity requires senior decision-makers to use data from continuous monitoring activities to make well-informed choices about the system's security posture and risk exposure.

Key Elements of Ongoing Authorization

- **Continuous Evaluation:** Conducts continuing analyses of security data to efficiently identify and manage system threats.

- **Adaptive Strategy:** Adjusts security measures and authorization status in response to evolving threats, weaknesses, and changes in the operational or threat landscape.

- **Proactive Decision Making:** Empowers executives to respond quickly in reaction to new security information, increasing the system's stability.

Objectives of Ongoing Authorization

- **Sustained Operational Clearance:** Ensures that the system continually fulfills the security requirements for continued operation.

- **Risk and Exposure Management:** Enables educated decision-making based on current information about the system's risk posture and vulnerability to threats.

- **Dynamic Security Posture:** This takes a flexible and responsive approach to security, allowing for quick alterations to meet new vulnerabilities and threats.

Importance of Task M-6

The completion of Task M-6 is essential for:

- **Maintaining System Integrity:** Ensures that operational technology systems continue to run within acceptable risk limits, hence protecting essential processes.

- **Enhancing System Resilience:** Task M-6 improves the overall reliability of operational technology systems by enabling quick reaction to security issues.

- **Supporting Proactive Risk Management:** Highlights the necessity of taking a proactive approach to managing security risks, ensuring that decision-makers can move quickly to update security measures and policies.

Task M-6, Ongoing Authorization, underlines the importance of continual evaluation and modification in the field of operational technology security. By enabling a dynamic approach to authorization and risk management, this role makes sure that systems stay safe in the face of increasing threats and operational changes. It demonstrates a commitment to proactive and informed security governance, which is essential for the protection and efficient functioning of critical infrastructure and technology systems.

6.54 TASK M-7: SYSTEM DISPOSAL

Task M-7, "System Disposal," focuses on the safe, responsible, and environmentally friendly disposal of operational technology (OT) systems. This assignment underlines the significance of carefully organizing the deconstruction or repurposing of technological components to secure sensitive data, comply with rules, and minimize environmental damage.

System Disposal Key Components

- **Viability Assessment:** Identifies which pieces can be reused, retired, recycled, or discarded.

- **Data Sanitization:** Uses comprehensive data destruction techniques to prevent unwanted access to sensitive information after disposal.

- **Environmental Consideration:** Implements methods for recycling or disposing of system components in ways that reduce negative environmental impacts.

Objectives of Task M-7

- **Data Security:** Ensures that any sensitive data stored in the system is permanently removed or destroyed to avoid data breaches.

- **Regulatory Compliance:** Follows legal and industry requirements for data privacy and environmental protection during the disposal procedure.

- **Environmental Responsibility:** Uses eco-friendly measures to lessen the environmental impact of disposing of technological systems.

Importance of Task M-7

The completion of Task M-7 is required for:

- **Maintaining Data Integrity:** Prevents the leaking of secret information throughout the system's disposal phase.

- **Legal and Ethical Compliance:** Ensures that disposal techniques comply with all applicable legal requirements and ethical concerns for data protection and environmental conservation.

- **Sustainable Technology Management:** Promotes responsible and sustainable methods in the management and termination of operational technology systems, in line with larger environmental goals.

Task M-7, System Disposal, highlights the importance of a systematic and precise approach to disposing of operating technological systems. This assignment provides a framework for responsibly completing the lifespan of OT systems by concentrating on safe data erasure, regulatory compliance, and sustainability. It represents a dedication to data protection, legal compliance, and environmental stewardship, ensuring that the disposal procedure is carried out with the highest caution and responsibility. This comprehensive plan not only meets immediate security and regulatory requirements, but it also matches global environmental sustainability goals, indicating a forward-thinking attitude to technology innovation and termination.

07 OT CYBER SECURITY ARCHITECTURE

7.1 INTRODUCTION: OT CYBERSECURITY ARCHITECTURE

This chapter delves into the Defense-in-Depth Architecture, which is a multi-layered strategic approach to cybersecurity. It is crafted to protect organizational systems by implementing several layers of security. Each of these layers caters to distinct security requirements, encompassing everything from physical security measures to network, and extending to software and hardware defenses. The key feature of this architecture is its redundancy; if a security breach occurs at one layer, subsequent layers continue safeguarding the fundamental systems. The value of this model is in its holistic defense mechanism, significantly bolstering resistance to cyber threats and reducing the risk of serious damage. For students, grasping this model is vital as it lays the groundwork for constructing durable cybersecurity defenses across different operational contexts, thus preserving the security and operational continuity of essential organizational functions.

7.2 DEFENSE-IN-DEPTH ARCHITECTURE

The Defense-in-Depth Architecture is a comprehensive cybersecurity architecture designed to protect enterprises with numerous levels of protection. This method is similar to an onion "Onion routing enhances anonymity by encrypting and routing internet traffic through multiple nodes", with several protective layers maintaining that if one barrier is penetrated, others remain to defend the center. The primary objective of this design is to delay illegal access and detect possible breaches before they cause major damage.

Overview of the Five Layers of Defense

Defense-in-Depth Architecture

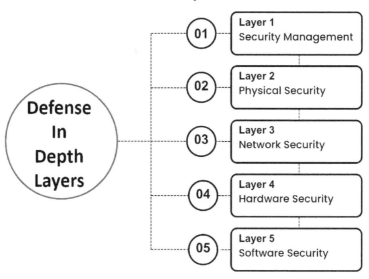

Layer 1: Security Management

- **Objective:** Build the security infrastructure by developing and enforcing security rules, processes, and overall governance.
- **Importance:** Serves as the foundation for the organization's security posture and strategic direction.

Layer 2: Physical Security

- **Objective:** Protect key hardware and facilities from physical attacks.
- **Function:** Uses physical barriers and controls to protect critical assets, assuring the safety of the organization's physical resources.

Layer 3: Network Security

- **Objective:** Aim to protect the infrastructure used for data transmission.
- **Methods:** Consists of employing firewalls, intrusion detection systems (IDS), intrusion prevention systems (IPS), and network segmentation to prevent unwanted access and assaults.

Layer 4: Hardware Security

- **Objective:** Protect physical devices against exploitation or modification.
- **Scope:** Focuses on the security of hardware components, specifically preventing unauthorized use or tampering.

Layer 5: Software Security

- **Objective:** Works to protect applications and operating systems by addressing software vulnerabilities.

- **Approach:** Involves intensive software testing, vulnerability eradication, and platform software enhancement to protect against external attacks.

The dynamic nature of the architecture

The Defense-in-Depth Architecture is intended to be dynamic, with continuous evaluations and modifications to handle new and growing cyber threats. Organizations may build an effective and adaptive security system that can protect against a wide range of attacks by strengthening each layer. This design highlights proactive and comprehensive cybersecurity rather than static asset defense, protecting both technology and human capital inside the business.

7.3 LAYER-1 SECURITY MANAGEMENT

In operational technology (OT) settings, security management is the foundation of a successful cybersecurity defensive plan. Positioned as the initial layer of a multi-tiered defensive architecture, Security Management plays an essential role in managing the strategic and organizational frameworks required for a strong security posture.

The Function of Security Management

- **Foundation of Defense:** Security Management is the basic layer upon which all other security measures are created and integrated.

- **Strategic Planning:** It includes the creation of complete policies, procedures, and systems to protect digital assets, assure operational continuity, and defend against known and undiscovered cyber threats.

- **Core Principle:** The idea of Security Management is to establish an integrated set of principles that lead and shape an organization's overall security strategy, aligning it with its overarching goals and risk tolerance.

Importance for OT Environments

Security Management plays an essential role in OT environments because individual operational needs have significant effects on security requirements. It not only defines the framework for securing critical infrastructure but also:

- **Customizes Security Measures:** Modifies security policies and processes to suit the specific features and weaknesses of OT systems.

- **Operational Integrity:** Ensures that security measures integrate smoothly with the principal functions of operational technology, preserving their integrity and effectiveness.

- **Adaptive and Responsive:** Allows for a dynamic security strategy that can respond to growing threats and operational changes, maintaining the OT environment's stability.

Security management is more than just a procedural requirement; it is a strategic compass that guides a company through the complicated environment of cybersecurity threats. Organizations may construct a solid basis for a multi-tiered defensive strategy by prioritizing the creation and deployment of an integrated Security Management layer, protecting their operational technology from an ever-changing array of cyber threats. This strategic layer establishes the groundwork for all other areas of cyber threat protection, assuring alignment with the organization's goals and tolerance for risk.

7.4 LAYER-2 PHYSICAL SECURITY

The importance of Physical Security as the second layer in a comprehensive defense-in-depth strategy cannot be highlighted in operational technology (OT). It is essential in safeguarding an organization's tangible assets and infrastructure against illegal access and physical threats.

Core Components of Physical Security

- **Physical Barriers:** The installation of physical barriers, such as fences, walls, and secure entrance points, is critical in preventing unwanted access. These barriers serve as the initial line of protection against attack.
- **Locking Mechanisms:** Enhanced security through secured doors and secure storage of important equipment while not in use adds an extra layer of protection.
- **Security Personnel:** The availability of alert security professionals to monitor and respond to suspected intrusions is important. They are the human component of the physical security layer, providing surveillance and fast-reaction capabilities.
- **Surveillance Technologies:** The use of real-time monitoring technology such as video surveillance and biometric verification systems facilitates the continuous observation of sensitive regions.
- **Access Control Systems:** Combining badge reading systems and electronic access controls with surveillance technology helps manage and record access to restricted locations.

Operational Importance

- **Asset Tracking:** A strong physical security infrastructure enables effective tracking of persons and high-value objects on the premises, assuring their safety.

- **Physical Intrusion Prevention:** By reinforcing the physical environment, companies may avoid intrusions that could lead to data theft or critical infrastructure damage.

- **Enhancing Overall Security Posture**: Implementing comprehensive physical security measures strengthens additional layers of protection, adding to the overall security posture of the OT environment.

Physical security is an integral component of a multi-layered defensive strategy, offering protection against physical threats to operational technological systems. Organizations may protect their physical assets and infrastructure by installing strong physical barriers, hiring security professionals, and using modern monitoring and access control technology, resulting in operational integrity and stability.

7.5 LAYER-3 NETWORK SECURITY

Network security is an essential component in protecting an organization's communication networks and data flow. It serves as a digital fortress, preventing cyber-attacks that seek to enter the network infrastructure, which is extremely important to the smooth functioning and integrity of operational technology (OT) systems.

Key Strategies for Enhancing Network Security

- **Segmentation and Isolation:** To improve network security, consider segmentation and isolation, dividing the network into secure segments restricts access and mitigates the impact of possible breaches, thereby controlling threats and restricting their propagation throughout the network.

- **Centralized Logging:** By centralizing log management, organizations may more effectively monitor network activities. This helps to recognize trends that indicate security breaches, allowing for more early detection and action.

- **Network Monitoring:** Continuous alertness through network monitoring is required. It involves examining network traffic to detect and proactively handle harmful activity, ensuring that the network is protected from unwanted access.

- **Malicious Code Protection:** Strong safeguards against malicious code are required. This involves implementing antivirus and anti-malware technologies to protect the network from different cyber threats, ensuring the network's integrity.

Operational Significance

- **Strengthening Network Defenses:** Creates a robust architecture to withstand cyber-attacks and ensure safe information flow.

- **Aligning with Cybersecurity Strategy:** Integrating network security measures into the organization's larger cybersecurity framework enables an integrated defense posture, which improves overall security.

- **Protecting the Attack Surface:** Because networks are frequently a key target for cyber assaults, improving network security is crucial for decreasing the organization's attack surface and protecting important operating technology.

Network security is an essential layer of defense in the cybersecurity architecture of operational technology. Organizations may build a reliable and powerful network architecture by strategically segmenting, actively monitoring, and implementing preventive measures against malicious code. This not only safeguards essential communication networks and data flow, but it also coincides with the organization's overall cybersecurity strategy by maintaining operational continuity and protecting against cyber-attacks.

7.6 NETWORK ARCHITECTURE

Operational Technology (OT) networks act as the foundation for modern industrial operations, allowing important procedures to run smoothly. The organization and security of these networks are essential necessitating a systematic approach to component classification and system isolation to protect data and functionality. This section looks into the layered security model and the concepts that support an effective OT network architecture.

Industrial Network Structure: Zones, Tiers, and Models

The classification of network components into layers, tiers, or zones is more than just an intellectual exercise; it is a practical need. The option to choose a risk-based implementation or a functional model determines the manner of isolation, to efficiently protect and manage network connections. The deliberate structuring of elements inside these zones is critical, guided by a thorough understanding of the system's daily performance, preventive security measures, and threat response.

Core Components of Network Architecture

To control traffic flow and assure segregation, the network structure incorporates a variety of hardware components such as switches, routers, and firewalls. This design not only protects against external attacks but also acts as an internal protection against potential system-wide disturbances.

Purdue Model of Control Hierarchy

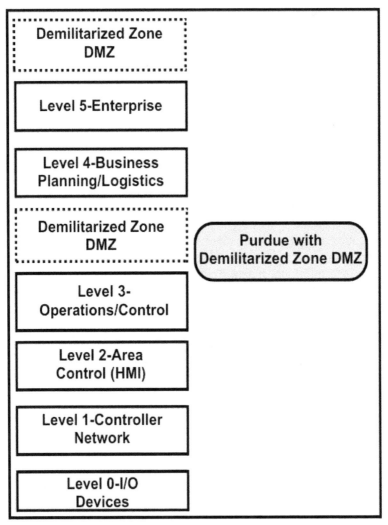

The Purdue Model provides a formal framework for structuring industrial control system architecture at several levels:

- **Level 0:** Field equipment, such as sensors and actuators, directly interact with the physical process.

- **Level 1:** Concentrates on controllers, generally programmable logic controllers (PLCs), which automate activities by interacting with Level 0 equipment.

- **Level 2:** Integrates supervisory control with interfaces for real-time process involvement and visibility.

- **Level 3:** Operations and control, including batch management and Supervisory Control and Data Acquisition SCADA for comprehensive process oversight.

- **Level 4:** Business planning and logistics, which involves analyzing operational data to make strategic company choices.

- **Level 5:** The highest level, which integrates business networks with the outside world.

Between levels 3 and 4, there is a demilitarized zone (DMZ) that protects industrial networks from external view while facilitating internal communication.

ISA/IEC 62443: Zone and Conduit Model

Zone and Conduit Model

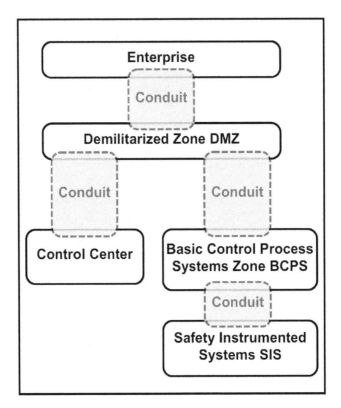

This model, which is aligned with the International Society of Automation/International Electrotechnical Commission ISA/IEC 62443 standards, divides industrial systems into zones with specific security needs.

- **Enterprise Zone:** Comprises of corporate systems and networks.
- **Demilitarized Zone (DMZ):** Serves as a buffer between the enterprise and industrial zones, ensuring important cross-zone communication.
- **Conduits:** Secure data channels governed by strict security regulations.
- **Control Center:** The operational core that includes process control and monitoring systems.
- **Basic Control Process Systems Zone:** Includes equipment required for direct industrial process control.
- **Safety Instrumented Systems (SIS):** Dedicated to operational safety and accident avoidance.

Organizations can develop a strong defense-in-depth strategy by using a systematic approach to network design that incorporates both the Purdue

Model and the Zone and Conduit model. This assures that a single failure is not detrimental to the entire network, protecting the integrity, availability, and confidentiality of control systems and data throughout the operational technology landscape against cyber-attacks.

7.7 CENTRALIZED LOGGING

Centralized logging is an essential component of improving an organization's network security. Organizations may considerably accelerate log management, strengthen cybersecurity efforts, and assure compliance with applicable laws by directing logs from various network components servers, routers, firewalls, and workstations to a single, centralized repository.

The Foundation of Centralized Logging

Centralized logging is essentially the collection of log data from across the network into a uniform storage system contained within the data center. This strategic approach has significance for various reasons:

- **Enhanced Log Analysis Efficiency:** By integrating logs, enterprises may better analyze data throughout their entire network, identifying trends and anomalies that may suggest cybersecurity concerns.

- **Improved Detection Capabilities:** Centralized logs make it easier to identify security breaches and unauthorized access attempts by offering a comprehensive picture of network activities.

- **Streamlined Storage and Retrieval:** A centralized log repository streamlines log data administration by making sure that logs are safely stored and easily accessible when required.

Implementing Centralized Logging

To successfully use centralized logging, organizations should:

- **Conduct a Comprehensive Assessment:** Determine the present condition of log management to verify that every important detail is correctly collected.

- **Customize Logging Practices:** Align logging operations with operational and cybersecurity requirements, and document every important occurrence.

- **Adhere to Policies and Regulations:** Ensure that internal and external logging and data preservation policies are followed, and that log data is both accurate and accessible.

Key Components of Centralized Logging

- **Firewalls:** Log network activity and possible threats to help detect and mitigate threats in real-time.

- **Servers:** Monitor login attempts and operation logs to detect unauthorized access and detrimental conduct.

- **Routers:** Monitor traffic flows and connections, giving information on traffic trends and network health.

- **Switches and Workstations:** Record device interactions and intrusion attempts, which are important in identifying and responding to security breaches.

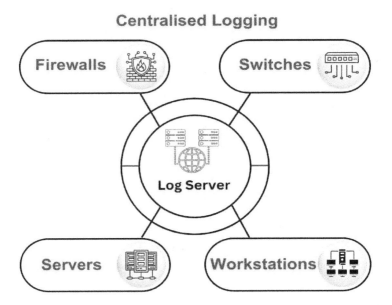

The Central Role of the Log Server

The log server is the core of the centralized logging system, collecting, managing, and analyzing logs from all across the network. The log server assures that:

- Logs are kept for just as long as required, following legal and regulatory obligations.

- There is enough storage space to store logs from all network components.

- Comprehensive log analysis helps to support compliance and forensic investigations.

Centralized logging is more than simply a security solution; it is a strategic approach to improving an organization's operational efficiency, security posture, and compliance. By deploying centralized logging, organizations can create a strong defensive system that effectively monitors and responds to network threats, assuring the protection of key digital assets and data.

7.8 NETWORK MONITORING

The "Network Monitoring" part focuses on advanced technologies used to monitor the flow of data within an organization, serving as an attentive digital guard over the company's data exchange. This method proves essential for detecting and mitigating security risks in real-time while also maintaining the integrity and confidentiality of business data.

Key Components of Network Monitoring

- **Behavior Anomaly Detection (BAD) Systems:** These systems are always alert, looking for any deviations from recognized patterns of activity that might signal a security concern. Their function is similar to checking for signals of problems and highlighting any activities that deviate from the usual.

- **Security Information and Event Management (SIEM) Systems:** SIEM systems are the statistical backbone of network monitoring, processing, and interpreting massive volumes of data provided by network security appliances. They play an important role in ensuring a safe environment by integrating various security events and alerts to detect possible attacks.

- **Intrusion Detection and Prevention Systems (IDS/IPS):** These devices, located at the network's entrance points, inspect all incoming and outgoing traffic. They are intended to identify and block efforts by malicious individuals to penetrate the network's defenses, serving as gatekeepers against malware and unauthorized access attempts.

Special Considerations for Operational Technology Networks

Intrusion Detection and Prevention IDS/IPS systems must be integrated into networks that govern industrial and manufacturing activities. These systems are capable of detecting both typical internet-based threats and OT communication irregularities such as Modbus and Distributed Network Protocol DNP3 protocols.

- **Challenges with Encrypted Traffic:** Monitoring messages that are encrypted involves several difficulties similar to trying to analyze bits of overheard conversations. The encrypted form of the data increases the possibility of false positives or missing detections.

Strategy for Effective Network Monitoring

Organizations must take a careful approach to effectively integrate these monitoring technologies into their operational frameworks. Organizations can improve their capacity to protect their digital infrastructure by aligning their systems to the exact encryption standards used on the network. This strategic integration assures that network monitoring tools are well-prepared to detect and respond to security threats, maintaining the organization's digital security posture.

Network monitoring in operational technology settings is a hard but necessary activity. Organizations may maintain watchful network supervision by utilizing BAD, SIEM, and IDS/IPS technologies. Companies can overcome the obstacles of encrypted traffic by carefully calibrating and integrating these systems, ensuring that their operational technologies are continuously protected against developing cybersecurity threats.

7.9 ZERO TRUST ARCHITECTURE

The Zero Trust Architecture (ZTA) is an architectural change in cybersecurity strategy, questioning the widely held idea that entities on an organization's network are naturally trustworthy. This strategy is based on the idea of "never trust, always verify," which requires thorough verification of all access requests, regardless of their origin.

Key Principles of Zero Trust Architecture

- **Never Trust, Always Verify:** Every entity, system, or network segment is addressed with suspicion, and all access requests are carefully reviewed.

- **Rigorous Identity Verification:** ZTA requires strong identity verification, making sure that access is only allowed to approved individuals.

- **Restrictive Access Policies:** Access is limited to what is essential, reducing the potential impact of breaches.

- **Continuous Validation:** The system regularly checks the security state of linked entities to detect and mitigate threats in real-time.

Challenges in Operations Technology (OT)

- **Latency Concerns:** In OT settings where activities are time-sensitive, authentication processes might cause delays.

- **Compatibility Issues:** Older OT technologies may lack the security measures required by a zero-trust framework.

- **Integration with IT:** The standard separation of IT and OT impacts the implementation of ZTA, necessitating a reconsideration of how security is managed throughout the enterprise.

Strategies to Overcome Implementation Barriers

- **Tailored Solutions:** Recognizing that there is no universal approach for deploying ZTA, organizations must create personalized strategies that take into consideration their specific operational needs.

- **Incremental Implementation:** Gradually adopting ZTA principles allows for modifications based on operational feedback, reducing interruptions.

- **Cultural and Organizational Change:** Transitioning to a zero-trust environment necessitates a fundamental transformation in corporate culture and practices, emphasizing the need for dynamic systems and a workforce that is sensitive to the new security perspective.

Implementing Zero Trust Architecture in Operational Technology presents unique concerns such as latency and compatibility with existing systems. Organizations can successfully handle these issues by taking a strategic approach that combines specialized solutions, planned adoption, and a concentration on cultural change. Using ZTA in OT settings improves security by implementing strict access restrictions and constant monitoring, lowering the risk of unauthorized access and the severity of possible security breaches.

7.10 LAYER-4 HARDWARE SECURITY

Hardware security is the fourth crucial layer in a complete defense-in-depth cybersecurity strategy. This layer supports the efficiency of both software and procedural protections by concentrating on the physical components of computer infrastructure. It plays an important role in developing confidence in an organization's technical architecture.

Fundamentals of Hardware Security

- **Trust in Physical and Virtualized Components:** Ensures that all hardware components, whether real or virtual, are legitimate and perform as intended.

- **Integrity Assurance:** Implements techniques to check the validity of hardware devices, offering they have not been tampered with and are functioning properly.

- **Access Control:** Restricts hardware operations to confirmed users, prohibiting unwanted access and modification.

- **Physical Tamper Resistant:** Prevents physical tampering and illegal access to hardware components.

- **Embedded Security and Encryption:** Technical protections like as Trusted Platform Modules (TPMs) and encryption protocols like Advanced Encryption Standard AES and Secure Hash Algorithm SHA, are used to improve system security and data protection.

Objectives of Hardware Security

The fundamental purpose of hardware security is to create trust in the system's hardware layer by providing that:

- **Hardware Authenticity:** All hardware components are original and have not been changed in any unlawful manner.

- **Predictable Behavior:** The hardware operates predictably under all operational settings, providing a solid basis for software and network security solutions.

- **Enhanced Endpoint Resistance:** Endpoints are reinforced against a wide range of cyber-attacks, decreasing physical technology stack weaknesses.

Implementing Hardware Security

To successfully deploy hardware security, organizations should:

- **Conduct Regular Hardware Audits:** Periodically evaluate and check hardware components for variations or evidence of tampering.

- **Apply Security Patches:** Regularly upgrade firmware and hardware drivers to resolve known vulnerabilities.

- **Utilize Secure Hardware Technologies:** Adopt hardware components that have security features like encryption and secure boot routines.

Hardware security is an important component in the defense-in-depth cybersecurity approach, highlighting the need to protect the physical components of IT infrastructure. Organizations can set the groundwork for greater cybersecurity measures by ensuring the integrity, authenticity, and secure functioning of their hardware. Implementing strong hardware security measures is a proactive way to reduce risks and improve the overall security posture of operational technology environments.

7.11 LAYER-5 SOFTWARE SECURITY

Software Security is the fifth and most important layer in the Defense-in-Depth architectural concept for operational technology (OT). This layer is responsible for preserving software applications and services that are important for OT systems, providing their secure and dependable functioning.

Software Security Best Practices

Application Allow listing

- **Purpose:** To prevent unauthorized software from being executed by only allowing approved software to operate.

- **Impact:** Improves security by restricting system functionality and reducing the possibility of illegal access and system harm.

Software Maintenance and Patching

- **Purpose:** Keep the software up to date and install updates regularly.

- **Strategy:** Addresses security vulnerabilities quickly and offers backup strategies for reverting updates if they interrupt the OT network.

Secure Software Development

- **Approach:** Integrates security procedures into the software development phase.

- **Method:** Uses audit testing and code reviews to reduce security risks throughout development, and to create software that prioritizes security.

Configuration Management

- **Goal:** To make sure that the software system is secure, manageable, and compliant with corporate requirements.
- **Practice:** Includes protecting apps and adjusting their setups to protect against potential attacks.

Objectives of Implementing Software Security

The overall purpose of implementing these software security principles is to:

- **Enhance Endpoint Security:** Organizations may protect their endpoints from cyber threats by ensuring that software is built, updated, and configured with security in mind.
- **Support OT Systems:** Effective software security measures improve the overall safety and dependability of OT systems, hence protecting important infrastructure.
- **Promote Organizational Safety:** By carefully implementing software security procedures, businesses may secure their operations from interruptions and cyber-attacks while retaining operational integrity.

The Software Security layer of the Defense-in-Depth approach serves as essential for securing the software that drives operational technology environments. Organizations may create a strong security posture by adopting tight allow listing, promising timely software maintenance, promoting safe development methods, and efficiently managing software settings. These activities together lead to a stronger and more reliable operational framework, which is essential in protecting OT systems from the changing perspective of cyber threats.

7.12 ADDITIONAL CONSIDERATION

Cybersecurity in the field of operational technology (OT) is a challenging environment that goes much beyond the scope of basic security measures. This complex sector demands a thorough evaluation of several undervalued components that together constitute the foundation of a strong defensive plan.

Key Elements of Cybersecurity in OT

Interaction Between Cyber Events and Protective Measures

- **Scenario:** Consider network disruptions activating fail-safe systems, resulting in shutdowns due to false emergency signals.
- **Objective:** Improve the accuracy of preventive measures and decrease false positives.

System Availability

- **Components:** Includes operational uptime, resistance to power interruptions, a variety of backup devices, and quick recovery strategies.
- **Goal:** Maintain continuous operations or quickly restore the system after a disturbance.

Compliance with the Regulatory Standards

- **Example:** The North American Electric Reliability Corporation adheres to Critical Infrastructure Protection requirements.
- **Purpose:** Protect the bulk electric system from cyber events that could negatively impact operations.

Environmental Considerations

- **Focus:** Identify and reduce eco-threats associated with cyber failures to avoid catastrophes.
- **Strategy:** Use architectural defenses to reduce environmental risks caused by system malfunctions.

Adaptation to Industrial Internet of Things (IIoT)

- **Challenge:** The challenge is to redefine system boundaries and service exposure as networked devices and sensors increase.
- **Solution:** Improve security for each potential vector created by IIoT integration.

End-to-End Encryption for Globally Distributed Systems

- **Requirement:** Secure all types of connections, including proximity, satellite, and internet-based communications.
- **Goal:** To protect data integrity and confidentiality across various communication networks.

Field I/O Security in Manufacturing Frameworks

- **Context:** Purdue Model Level 0 focuses on the security of communication drivers and devices that interface directly with physical processes.
- **Problem:** Reduce low levels of identification in sensors and actuators to prevent illegal access and manipulation.

Navigating the cybersecurity landscape in OT needs a comprehensive, multifaceted strategy that involves several organizational and technological areas. The path to securing OT ecosystems requires not only the implementation of advanced security measures, but also a thorough understanding of the interconnectedness of cyber events, system availability, regulatory compliance, environmental safety, IIoT integration, and field I/O device protection. This comprehensive strategy is essential for maintaining the security integrity of OT systems and ensuring their resistance to an ever-changing range of cyber threats.

7.13 DISTRIBUTED CONTROL SYSTEM (DCS)-BASED OT SYSTEM

The Defense-in-Depth architecture is a strong multi-layered technique for protecting Operational Technology (OT) systems, particularly Distributed Control Systems (DCS), by creating numerous layers of security defenses. Each layer handles a distinct aspect of protection, adding to the overall strength of the OT environment.

Distributed Control System (DCS)-Based OT Systems

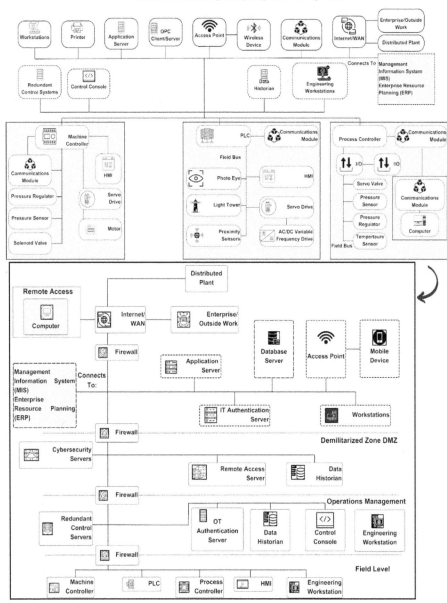

Framework Layers

Layer 1: Security Management

- **Purpose:** Create careful security management procedures, including risk assessments, user role descriptions, and breach response methods.

- **Function:** Lays the groundwork for the security strategy, assuring readiness for any security breaches within the DCS environment.

Layer 2: Physical Security

- **Focus:** Increases physical security measures for OT systems beyond typical locks and obstacles.

- **Measures:** Includes biometric scan-based access control to important places and environmental protection for sensitive equipment.

Layer 3: Network Security

- **Goal:** Protect the DCS network infrastructure from cyber-attacks.

- **Strategies:** Involve dividing the network, installing firewalls, and using intrusion prevention/detection systems to safeguard network perimeters and interior segments.

Layer 4: Hardware Security

- **Objective:** Protect physical equipment that is essential to the OT system and DCS operations.

- **Approach:** Protects hardware from tampering and illegal substitution to prevent DCS network outages.

Layer 5: Software Security

- **Objective:** Ensure that DCS software is protected against viruses and unauthorized modification.

- **Implementation:** Uses application allowlisting to prevent illegal applications from compromising the DCS.

DCS Control Cascade Hierarchy

The DCS control cascade hierarchy is consistent with the Defense-in-Depth layers, demonstrating how centralized digital controls interact with machinery at the lowest tiers. This hierarchical organization aids decision-making at the operational and strategic levels:

- **Operational level:** At the operational level, direct engagement with machine controls assures that manufacturing processes continue or stop.

- **Management Level:** Control systems, sometimes known as intermediate levels of defense, are used by operators and engineers to make production-related decisions.

- **Strategic Level:** Data and reports from lower Defense-in-Depth levels feed high-level decisions, ensuring that they are in line with the organization's overall goals.

The Defense-in-Depth structure assures that a breach in one area is not detrimental to the entire DCS system by layering tactics that retain the OT system's internal integrity in the event of a specific layer breach. This complete strategy not only defends against external attacks but also maintains the DCS's operational integrity, allowing the system to run successfully even in the face of security issues.

7.14 DCS/PLC-BASED OT WITH IIOT

Operational Technology (OT) environments, particularly those involving Distributed Control Systems (DCS) and Programmable Logic Controllers (PLC), are developing with a decentralization focus. This change allows for complete control approaches over large-scale processes, similar to considering the entire production system as a single infrastructure. The addition of the Industrial Internet of Things (IIoT) to these frameworks enhances their capabilities by providing vast connection and data analysis capabilities.

DCS/PLC-Based OT with IIoT

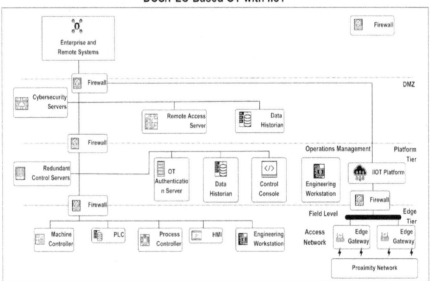

Key Components and Functions

- **Network Segmentation:** To ensure seamless operations, IoT devices are separated into appropriate network segments. This separation ensures that IIoT device activities do not disrupt the fundamental functionality of DCS/PLC systems.

- **IIoT Platform Layer:** Serves as a conduit for communication between IoT devices and the larger network, supported by a secure Demilitarized Zone (DMZ) to defend against external attacks.

- **Demilitarized Zone (DMZ):** Acts as a regulated middleman, allowing external access to specific OT services while protected by strong firewalls.

- **Servers and Data Historians:** These parts, located within the DMZ, allow for remote access and analysis of operational data, providing a secure connection within the operational network.

- **Enterprise Level to Field Level Connection:** Uses the DMZ as a secure bridge to connect the enterprise's top-layer operational management devices with field-level devices.

- **Edge Devices:** From sophisticated sensors to complicated actuators, these field-level devices send real-time data to the control system and, in some cases, receive operational instructions.

Security and Management with IIoT Integration

Integrating IIoT into OT systems demands careful supervision of new components, highlighting the need for:

- **Secured Communication:** All IIoT communication is conducted through DMZ border firewalls, which improves monitoring and control over interactions between IIoT components and the main system.

- **Risk Mitigation:** This organized technique enables complete examination and regulation of interactions, lowering the likelihood of cyber-attacks that could damage system integrity.

The suggested system highlights a strategic balance between improving connectivity and ensuring security in current industrial processes. By incorporating IIoT, operational technology systems not only improve their data integration and analytical capabilities but also maintain the strict safety and reliability requirements required in OT environments. This balanced approach highlights the need for advanced network architecture and security management in the modern age of smart industrial processes.

7.15 SCADA-BASED OT ENVIRONMENTS

Supervisory Control and Data Acquisition (SCADA) systems are necessary for monitoring and regulating industrial processes and critical infrastructure. These systems collect insights from sensors spread across several areas and compile this information into a single system to accurately direct activities. SCADA systems' underlying susceptibility to cyber-attacks needs a strong, multi-layered security strategy known as defense-in-depth. This strategy integrates security mechanisms across several IT landscape levels to properly protect SCADA settings.

SCADA-Based OT Environments

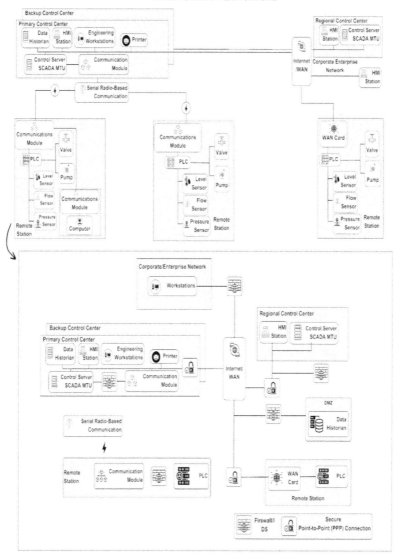

Defense-in-Depth Layers in SCADA System

- **Layer 1: Security Management:** This fundamental layer sets the SCADA system's security regulations and protocols, as well as user roles, access rights, and security recommendations.

- **Layer 2 - Physical Security:** This layer is important for avoiding physical tampering with SCADA equipment and comprises gate security, premises monitoring, surveillance cameras, and alarm systems.

- **Layer 3 - Network Security:** Secures data transmission over SCADA networks using firewalls, intrusion detection systems, and network segmentation to distinguish between corporate and control networks.

- **Layer 4 - Hardware Security:** Concentrates on protecting SCADA hardware components, such as servers, workstations, and other key devices, and ensuring they meet security requirements.

- **Layer 5 - Software Security:** Ensures the security of software programs from development to maintenance and upgrades, protecting against vulnerabilities.

SCADA System Architecture and Control

The essence of SCADA systems resides in industrial process control, carried out by:

- **Main Control Center:** Oversees real-time data collecting and process control.

- **Regional Control Centers:** Manage several local locations, including backup centers to increase system resilience.

- **Remote Stations:** Equipped with Programmable Logic Controllers (PLCs) for local process control and data transfer to central and regional decision-making centers.

Network Communications and Security

The communication structure of SCADA systems is carefully constructed to prevent unwanted access, particularly when control centers are linked to corporate networks. This comprises secure communication lines between distant stations, control centers, and regional hubs to assure data integrity and system security.

A defense-in-depth strategy is a necessity for SCADA systems since it provides a comprehensive security barrier against both external and internal threats. This technique assures that the system operates continuously while protecting the confidentiality, availability, and integrity of crucial industrial control systems. SCADA systems may function effectively and safely when various levels of security are integrated, especially in the face of growing cyber threats.

08 OT SECURITY CAPABILITIES AND TOOLS

8.1 INTRODUCTION: OT SECURITY TOOLS AND CAPABILITIES

This chapter explores sophisticated strategies for network segmentation, essential for boosting security in Operational Technology (OT). It discusses the implementation and advantages of various segmentation tools such as firewalls, unidirectional gateways, Virtual Local Area Networks (VLANs), and Software Defined Networking (SDN), following the guidelines of the National Institute of Standards and Technology (NIST) SP 800-82. The significance of these methods is their capability to safeguard OT environments by managing and restricting network traffic, thereby improving overall security measures. For students, mastering these technologies is vital as it provides them with the necessary skills to develop, deploy, and manage secure network frameworks in industrial contexts, protecting vital infrastructure against contemporary cybersecurity risks.

8.2 SEGMENTATION – FIREWALL

Operational Technology (OT) systems, essential for controlling industrial processes, have been increasingly integrated into Information Technology (IT) networks. This integration increases productivity while potentially exposing Operational Technology (OT) to various security challenges. Relying on National Institute of Standards and Technology NIST SP 800-82 principles, this enhanced guide goes into the complex methods and tools required for resilient OT security, with a focus on a multi-layered defense mechanism known as Defense-in-Depth.

In-Depth Analysis of Firewall Technologies:

Firewalls act as sensors at the network's edge, separating safe internal networks from possibly adversarial exterior ones. Their intelligence ranges, according to various operating requirements:

- **Basic Packet Filtering Firewalls:** These fundamental firewalls check each data packet against a set of requirements, such as permitted IP addresses and Transmission Control Protocol/User Datagram Protocol TCP/UDP ports, to enable or deny traffic. They operate at the OSI model's network (Layer 3) and transport (Layer 4) levels and are quick, but lack context about the traffic's status or session.

- **Stateful Inspection Firewalls:** These firewalls go beyond simple packet filtering to investigate the status and context of active connections. They monitor the progress of each session, allowing them to make better judgments regarding traffic flow and provide greater security.

- **Next-Generation Firewalls (NGFWs):** These firewalls have advanced capabilities including deep packet inspection, application-level inspection, and integrated intrusion prevention systems. NGFWs provide detailed management and protection by knowing the programs and people that use the network, which is important in today's complex cyber threat landscape.

In the field of OT, where system integrity and availability are crucial firewalls serve an essential role in enforcing network segmentation and protecting sensitive control systems from unwanted access.

Increasing OT Security Capabilities and Tools

Securing OT systems goes beyond network segmentation and involves a set of techniques and tools:

Strategic Network Segmentation and Isolation

- **Physical and Logical Separation:** Organizations can construct separated network segments by using firewalls, unidirectional gateways (data diodes), and sophisticated networking techniques like Virtual LANs (VLANs) and Software-Defined Networking (SDN). This not only reduces the attack surface but also limits the propagation of any security breaches.

Enhanced Network Monitoring and SIEM

- **Centralized Logging and Active Monitoring:** Organizations can evaluate and correlate network events by collecting logs from diverse sources (e.g., firewalls, routers, servers) and storing them in a single repository. Real-time monitoring, threat detection, and incident response rely heavily on tools such as Security Information and Event Management (SIEM).

- **Malware and Anomaly Detection:** Using IDS/IPS (Intrusion Detection Systems/Intrusion Prevention Systems) and behavioral analytics to look for unexpected patterns that might indicate a cyber attack. These technologies serve as essential for early identification and reaction to suspected security breaches.

Strict Data Security Practices

- **Robust Backup and Encryption:** Using safe backup storage systems and encryption to protect data at rest and in transit. These steps protect data integrity and confidentiality, which is crucial in the case of a data breach or system intrusion.

- **Configuration Management and Secure Software Practices:** Ensures that all software on OT devices is constantly updated and patched. Use safe development methods to reduce vulnerabilities in the software that runs on OT devices.

Implementing a Zero Trust Architecture in OT Environments

The Zero Trust Architecture (ZTA) symbolizes an important shift in cybersecurity by promoting the notion of "never trust, always verify." In OT situations, this implies that every access request, whether from within the internal network or from outside, is carefully verified. Implementing ZTA in OT contexts necessitates solving specific issues, such as reducing latency in control systems and preserving compatibility with older technology.

The security of OT systems from cyber attacks is a complex and dynamic task. Organizations may strengthen their OT environments by implementing a Defense-in-Depth strategy, including modern firewall technologies, and using a complete set of security capabilities and tools. Adherence to standards such as NIST SP 800-82, continuous monitoring, and a proactive approach to cybersecurity can help protect critical infrastructure from evolving threats while assuring operational resilience and continuity.

8.3 SEGMENTATION - UNIDIRECTIONAL GATEWAY

Operational Technology (OT) solutions are essential for regulating industrial and infrastructure operations. Ensuring the security of these systems is essential, particularly in industries such as electricity generation, where breaches can have serious effects. The unidirectional gateway, often known as a data diode because of its one-way data transmission capacity, is an essential technology in protecting these settings. This section examines the relevance, functionality, and components of unidirectional gateways, focusing on their implementation within the context of NIST SP 800-82 principles.

Significance of Unidirectional Gateways

Unidirectional gateways are necessary in contexts that require strict data integrity and secrecy. These devices have an important role in safeguarding OT systems because they allow data to flow in just one direction, which helps to mitigate external cyber risks.

Working of Unidirectional Gateways

Unidirectional Gateways

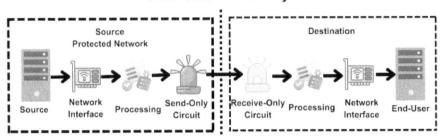

A unidirectional gateway's principal role is to enable safe data transfer from a protected network to an external destination while minimizing the possibility of illegal inbound traffic. This operation is accomplished using various components:

- **Source (Protected Network):** The origin of sensitive or operational data that has to be shared with others.

- **Send-Only Circuit:** Enables data transfer outside of the protected network. Its architecture prevents it from receiving incoming data, so generating a secure perimeter.

- **Receive-Only Circuit:** Located at the receiving end, it is set to only accept data from the protected network, preventing data from being transmitted back.

- **Destination (External Network):** The data's endpoint, such as a monitoring system or analytics platform does not require data to be sent to the protected network.

Application and Implementation

Unidirectional gateways are particularly valuable in situations when network integrity and availability exceed the necessity for bidirectional communication. This is frequently the case in important infrastructure, where a cyber breach can have far-reaching physical implications. Implementing these gateways adheres to risk management standards, protecting high-priority systems from unwanted access while ensuring essential information flow to promote operational efficiency.

Unidirectional gateways represent a proactive approach to cybersecurity in OT environments, allowing safe data delivery while preventing potential inbound threats. By incorporating these devices into OT security policies, organizations could enhance critical system protection against sophisticated cyber incidents, following the best practices stated in NIST SP 800-82. This strategic deployment highlights the significance of stacking protection measures to protect OT systems from emerging cyber threats.

8.4 SEGMENTATION - VIRTUAL LOCAL AREA NETWORKS

Virtual Local Area Networks (VLANs) play a crucial role in the network architecture and security framework within Operational Technology (OT) environments. These networks are instrumental in logically segmenting network traffic, which is vital for maintaining the integrity, security, and efficiency of operations. This discussion delves into the purpose of VLANs, provides examples of their configuration, and explores their alignment with the guidelines set forth in NIST SP 800-82 for protecting Industrial Control Systems (ICS).

Introduction to VLANs: VLANs facilitate the logical division of network traffic within a singular physical infrastructure. This division allows devices connected to the same physical switch to operate as if they were part of separate, isolated networks. This virtual separation is essential for creating specific broadcast domains, which enhances network management and bolsters security.

Example of VLAN Configuration: Take the case of an 8-port switch divided into two VLANs:

- **Ports 1-4:** Designated for VLAN A, where devices on these ports communicate as though they were in an independent network.

- **Ports 5-8:** Assigned to VLAN B, where devices function within their own network realm. This configuration exemplifies how VLANs segregate network traffic to foster greater confidentiality and operational efficiency across different departments or operational zones.

Network Diagram and VLAN Implementation

A network with three switches linked to a single router, each corresponding to a separate VLAN Engineering, Marketing, and Accounting, shows VLANs in operation. This configuration highlights VLANs' ability to separate departmental traffic, ensuring that each department's network communication is kept secret and secure from others.

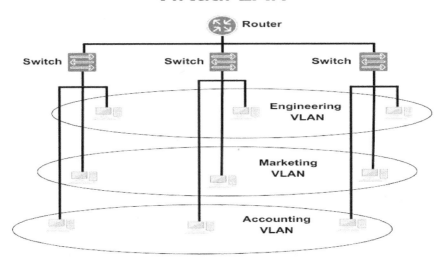

VLANs in the NIST SP 800-82 Context

According to NIST SP 800-82, which focuses on Industrial Control Systems ICS security, VLANs serve an important role in accomplishing network segmentation, a basic security method.

Key advantages include:

- **Separation of ICS and Corporate Networks:** VLANs can separate sensitive ICS networks from regular corporate networks, lowering the possibility of unauthorized access to important systems.

- **Isolation within ICS:** Critical devices and systems can be isolated to specific VLANs, reducing the attack surface and improving security.

- **Access Control:** VLANs offer role-based access control, making sure that users only access network segments that are required for their responsibilities, so reflecting the concept of least privilege.

VLANs are an essential element of modern OT network security, providing a flexible and efficient method for logically segmenting networks. This segmentation not only increases security but also improves network speed and simplifies management. Organizations that align VLAN installation with NIST SP 800-82 standards can significantly minimize risks to their OT and ICS settings, protecting critical infrastructure from cyber-attacks. VLANs are an example of a proactive security measure that is essential to a defense-in-depth approach and the foundation of strong OT security frameworks.

8.5 SEGMENTATION - SOFTWARE DEFINED NETWORKING

Software-defined networking (SDN) is an innovative approach to network management that provides significant benefits for protecting Operational Technology (OT) settings. This section goes into the SDN architecture, comparing it to older networking techniques, and explains its merits in the context of OT security, with a focus on matching with NIST SP 800-82 guidelines for Industrial Control Systems security.

Understanding SDN Architecture

SDN transforms traditional networking by separating the control plane (decision-making component) from the data plane (packet forwarding component) of network devices such as switches and routers. This division makes it easier to administer networks centrally, giving you more dynamic and flexible control over data flows.

- **Traditional vs. SDN Architecture:** Traditional networks include both control and data planes embedded in each device, limiting network administration and adaptability to changing requirements. In contrast, SDN centralizes the control plane in a single controller, simplifying network design and maintenance.

- **Centralized Control Plane:** The SDN controller acts as the network's brain, allowing administrators to oversee traffic flow throughout the whole network from a single interface. This centralization makes network modifications easier, increases visibility, and improves the network's responsiveness to changes.

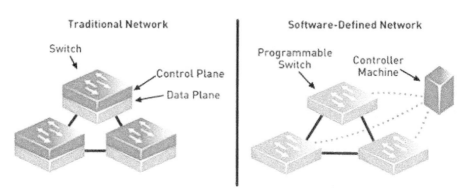

Advantages of SDN in Operational Technology

- **Network Flexibility and Agility:** SDN's centralized administration enables quick reconfiguration of network settings to meet changing needs, improve security, or respond to events.

- **Improved Security Posture:** By dynamically segmenting the network, SDN helps to create safe zones and channels, hence increasing the network's resistance to attacks and unauthorized access.

- **Efficient Incident Response:** SDN allows for faster isolation of affected devices and redirection of traffic for analysis, enhancing the organization's capacity to mitigate and respond to cyber events.

Aligning SDN with NIST SP 800-82 guidelines

NIST SP 800-82 describes solutions for protecting industrial control systems, several of which can be efficiently implemented by employing SDN:

- **Security Zones and Conduits:** SDN enables the dynamic establishment and maintenance of security zones, following NIST SP 800-82's guidelines for separating control system networks from corporate networks.

- **Centralized Security Administration:** The SDN controller provides a single point for setting and enforcing security policies throughout the network, simplifying security administration.

- **Rapid Threat Adaptation:** Because SDN is programmable, network settings may be adjusted quickly in reaction to discovered threats or weaknesses, improving the entire security framework of OT environments.

Software-defined networking is a fundamental shift in how networks are managed and secured, especially in the context of operational technology. SDN corresponds with and supports the security concepts stated in NIST SP 800-82, providing an effective foundation for safeguarding important industrial control systems against changing cyber threats. This chapter focuses on SDN's ability to rethink network security policies, assuring operational integrity and resilience in the face of advanced cyber threats.

8.6 NETWORKING MONITORING / SECURITY INFORMATION AND EVENT MANAGEMENT – BEHAVIOR ANOMALY DETECTION / DATA LOSS PREVENTION

Operational Technology (OT) systems, which regulate and monitor industrial processes, present particular cybersecurity issues. These essential infrastructures rely heavily on advanced security techniques such as Behavior Anomaly Detection (BAD), Data Loss Prevention (DLP), and Security Information and Event Management (SIEM) systems. This section examines these procedures in depth, matching with the principles outlined in NIST SP 800-82 for improving OT security.

Behavior Anomaly Detection (BAD)

BAD systems are important for detecting possible security issues that depart from established network standards.

- **Baseline Comparison:** BAD systems assess network activity by comparing it to a specified baseline that represents normal operations. This method proves essential for detecting variations that may suggest cybersecurity risks or operational irregularities.

- **Detection Mechanism:** Anomalies such as strange traffic patterns, new protocol use, or unexpected device interactions cause alarms. These occurrences that deviate from the baseline are investigated for any security concerns.

- **AI and ML Integration:** By incorporating artificial intelligence and machine learning, these systems can continuously develop and update their baseline models. This flexibility is essential in recognizing between harmless changes in network activity and significant risks.

Data Loss Prevention (DLP)

DLP systems secure sensitive data by preventing unwanted access and extraction.

- **Core Functionality:** DLP systems protect data at rest and in transit, addressing risks associated with unlawful data management and transfer.

- **SIEM Synergy:** Integrating DLP with SIEM systems provides a full security picture by combining data protection and extensive network surveillance.

Security Information and Event Management (SIEM)

SIEM systems combine many security mechanisms to provide real-time monitoring and incident response capabilities.

Centralized Logging: Combining logs from several sources into a single repository allows for extensive analysis and correlation, promoting a coordinated response to security problems.

Scanning Methods

- **Passive Scanning:** Evaluates network traffic to find vulnerabilities without affecting operations.

- **Active Scanning:** Rapidly tracks for exploitable vulnerabilities throughout the network.

- **Malware and Anomaly Detection:** SIEM systems detect the spread of malware throughout the network as well as irregularities that indicate possible security breaches.

NIST SP 800-82 and OT Security

NIST SP 800-82 recommends applying enhanced security measures in OT settings.

- **BAD's Role:** In the context of Industrial Control Systems (ICS), BAD assists in identifying complex risks such as Advanced Persistent Threats (APTs) and insider actions, that typical security technologies may not detect.

- **DLP Importance:** Due to the sensitive nature of operational data, DLP methods have significance for preventing data breaches that might affect critical facilities.

- **SIEM Recommendations:** Tailored SIEM solutions for ICS are recommended, since they are capable of analyzing unique network traffic and events common in such environments, allowing for swift threat identification and response.

Adopting advanced security measures such as BAD, DLP, and SIEM following NIST SP 800-82 recommendations improves OT systems' resistance to changing cybersecurity threats. When these technologies are properly integrated, they provide a strong defensive mechanism that protects essential systems from possible attacks while assuring operational continuity.

8.7 NETWORKING MONITORING / SIEM - DECEPTION & DIGITAL TWIN

Operational Technology (OT) environments, which are essential for controlling and monitoring industrial operations, are rapidly incorporating modern technologies to improve security and efficiency. This section goes into the application of Digital Twins and Deception Technology in OT contexts, following the concepts described in NIST SP 800-82 for protecting Industrial Control Systems (ICS).

Digital Twins in OT

Concept Overview: A digital twin is a complex virtual clone of a physical system or component that is constantly updated with real-time sensor data to properly represent its counterpart's status.

Operational Benefits

- **Performance Monitoring:** Allows for continuous observation of system performance, supporting condition-based maintenance.

- **Anomaly Detection:** Uses machine learning techniques to identify deviations from typical operations, which may indicate maintenance needs or system problems.

Cybersecurity Enhancements

- **Early Warning System:** Serves as an initial-line detection system for cybersecurity incidents, recognizing abnormalities that may bypass standard security procedures.

Deception Technology for Cybersecurity

- **Defensive Strategy:** Uses decoys or honeypots to impersonate authentic network assets to lure and redirect attackers away from actual targets.

Tactical Advantages

- **Intrusion Detection:** When an attacker engages with a decoy, notifications are sent to cybersecurity professionals, informing them of possible breaches.
- **Intelligence Gathering:** Enables the monitoring of attacker activities, providing insights into harmful methods, and permitting rapid threat response.

Alignment with NIST SP 800-82

Digital twins

- **Continuous Monitoring:** Builds on NIST's guideline for continuous monitoring of industrial control system ICS activities, improving the identification and reaction to operational and security problems.

Deception technology

- **Defense-in-Depth:** Complements the NIST's multi-layered security strategy by providing a misleading layer to enhance defense against cyber-attacks.

Integrating Digital Twins and Deception Technology into the OT security architecture greatly enhances the resistance of industrial control system ICS against malicious attackers. Digital Twins provides a proactive approach to system maintenance and anomaly detection, whilst Deception Technology adds a unique layer of security by deceiving attackers and enabling in-depth threat research. Together, these technologies are an essential element of NIST SP 800-82's comprehensive security approach for protecting the integrity, availability, and confidentiality of important industrial processes. This strategic alignment not only strengthens OT environments against current cyber threats but also sets the path for future advances in industrial cybersecurity standards.

8.8 DATA SECURITY – IMMUTABLE STORAGE / HASHING

Operational Technology (OT) systems are fundamental to the operation of crucial facilities, necessitating strong security measures to protect against cyber-attacks. Following the NIST SP 800-82 recommendations, this section analyzes the use of Immutable Storage, File Hashing, and Block Ciphers to improve OT security.

Immutable Storage: Ensures data integrity

- **Definition:** Immutable storage is a data preservation technology that prevents revisions after data has been saved, which is essential for preserving backup data from tampering or illegal changes.

- **Operational Use:** Immutable storage is ideal for keeping safe copies of important system information, such as software and configuration data, and it improves disaster recovery by assuring the availability of clean backup data.

- **Security Advantage:** This storage mechanism protects against the risks associated with illegal software installations by using its read-only nature to improve system security.

File Hashing: Integrity Verification

- **Process Overview:** File hashing uses a hash function to obtain a unique hash value from a file's contents, which serves as a digital fingerprint to verify data integrity.

- **Change Detection:** Any alteration to a file affects its hash value, making file hashing an effective technique for detecting illegal modifications and potential security breaches.

- **Application:** Hash values play an important role in preserving file system security, particularly in identifying tampering or illegal adjustments that indicate cybersecurity issues.

Block Ciphers: Confidentiality through Encryption

- **Encryption Methodology:** Block ciphers encrypt data in fixed-size blocks, making it easier to secure huge datasets and protect sensitive information.

- **Operational Significance:** By encrypting data at rest in blocks, block ciphers serve an important role in preventing unwanted access to essential information, in line with data security best practices.

- **Security Enhancement:** This encryption strategy plays an important role in ensuring data integrity and confidentiality, and it serves as the foundation of complete OT security initiatives.

Alignment with NIST SP 800-82

- **Immutable Storage:** Adheres to NIST requirements for safe data backups, enabling excellent disaster recovery and system resilience.

- **File Hashing:** Matches NIST's focus on integrity checks to detect illegal alterations, providing a proactive approach to cyber threats.

- **Block Ciphers:** Implements NIST's cryptographic standards for protecting sensitive data, maintaining confidentiality, and securing OT environments against unwanted exposure.

Incorporating Immutable Storage, File Hashing, and Block Ciphers into OT security frameworks greatly improves significant systems' defenses against growing cyber threats. Organizations that follow NIST SP 800-82 principles can safeguard the integrity, availability, and confidentiality of their OT systems, improving overall operational resilience and security. These solutions provide a solid foundation for establishing a security-conscious culture in OT settings, assuring the long-term safety and dependability of important infrastructure components.

8.9 DATA SECURITY - DIGITAL SIGNATURES / REMOTE ACCESS

In the field of operational technology (OT), protecting communications and remote access to Industrial Control Systems (ICS) is necessary. Following the recommendations outlined in NIST SP 800-82, this section looks into the use of Digital Signatures and Remote Access over VPNs to improve ICS security.

Digital Signature: Authenticity and Integrity

Core Function: Digital signatures are cryptographic methods that secure the integrity and validity of digital information by serving as the electronic substitute for a handwritten signature.

Key Benefits

- **Verification:** They check the signatory's identity and certify that the content has not been changed after signing.

- **Non-Repudiation:** Verify the message's origin and integrity, making sure that the sender cannot challenge the legitimacy of the sent information.

- **Implementation:** Digital signatures use public key infrastructure (PKI) to enable secure transactions, making them important in safeguarding ICS communications.

- **NIST SP 800-82 Guidance:** Supports the use of digital signatures in ICS communications to prevent tampering and authenticate data sources.

- **Remote Access Using VPN:** VPNs provide safe connectivity by creating an encrypted route over potentially insecure networks such as the Internet. This ensures data confidentiality and integrity while in transmission.

Operational Importance

- **Secure Remote Access:** Enables secure access to network resources from remote locations, which is important for ICS control and monitoring.

- **Data Protection:** Encrypts data transfer to prevent interception and unwanted access.

- **NIST Recommendations:** Promotes VPNs for secure remote ICS access, highlighting their role in providing strong authentication and encryption to protect control systems from external threats.

Integrating Security Measures

NIST SP 800-82 recommends both digital signatures and VPNs as part of a complete ICS security policy. These technologies provide crucial security against cyber threats to operational systems by maintaining data integrity, authenticating users, and securing network communications.

- **Layered Security Model:** Follows NIST's multi-layered security strategy, using several defense mechanisms to reduce distinct cyber threats.

- **Contribution to ICS Security:** These steps improve the security posture of ICS by safeguarding data flows and enabling safe remote operations, in line with best practices for protecting critical infrastructure.

The use of digital signatures and VPNs plays an important role in protecting ICS against cyber threats. According to NIST SP 800-82, these technologies provide a strong framework for securing ICS communications and remote access, maintaining operational continuity, and protecting critical infrastructure. This strategic use of cryptographic verification and secure connection underlines the importance of a proactive approach to cybersecurity in the operational technology domain.

CHAPTER

09 CONCLUSION

As we wrap up this comprehensive exploration of Operation Technology and the NIST Cybersecurity Framework, we (both authors — Bipin and Anand) sincerely hope that the information we shared here, has not only served as a guide for you, but also ignited your passion for Operation technology and encouraged you to enhance cybersecurity measures in your work. Throughout this book, we've attempted to demystified complex OT concepts and provided actionable insights, empowering you to strengthen your defences against ever-evolving cyber threats.

If you have any questions or need further assistance navigating the complexities of Operation Technology or NIST CSF Framework, don't hesitate to reach out to any of the authors. Both authors are easily accessible via LinkedIn or their websites. Both of us are committed to supporting your journey toward a more secure cyber environment and are eager to offer guidance.

Additionally, we would love to connect with you professionally on LinkedIn, where we regularly share valuable information, updates, and the latest news about cybersecurity and Operation Technology. Our posts are designed to keep OT enthusiasts informed and ahead in the field.

For those seeking career guidance in this dynamic industry, Anand Shinde, a seasoned career counsellor and mentor, is here to help. He collaborates with universities and educational institutions, passionate about nurturing the next generation of cybersecurity professionals. If you're considering a career in this field or need advice, feel free to contact him directly.

Lastly, we encourage you to share your feedback on this book and spread the knowledge you've gained to fellow enthusiasts in the field of Operation Technology. Your insights and engagement contribute significantly to our shared goal of creating a safer, more secure digital world.

www.ingramcontent.com/pod-product-compliance
Lightning Source LLC
LaVergne TN
LVHW022344060326
832902LV00022B/4230